FrontPage 2000

Thomas Guillemain

Prentice Hall

An imprint of PEARSON EDUCATION

PEARSON EDUCATION LIMITED

Head Office:
Edinburgh Gate
Harlow
Essex CM20 2JE
Tel: +44 (0)1279 623623
Fax: +44 (0)1279 431059

London Office:
128 Long Acre
London WC2E 9AN
Tel: +44 (0)207 447 2000
Fax: +44 (0)207 240 5771

First published in Great Britain 2000

© Pearson Education Limited 2000

First published in 1999 as
Se Former En Un Jour: FrontPage 2000
by CampusPress France
19, rue Michel Le Comte
75003 Paris
France

Library of Congress Cataloging in Publication Data
Available from the publisher.

British Library Cataloguing in Publication Data
A CIP catalogue record for this book can be obtained from the British Library.

ISBN 0-13-016223-x

All rights reserved. No part of this publication may be reproduced, stored
in a retrieval system, or transmitted, in any form, or by any means, electronic,
mechanical, photocopying, recording or otherwise, without prior permission,
in writing, from the publisher.

10 9 8 7 6 5 4 3 2 1

Translated and typeset by Cybertechnics, Sheffield.
Printed and bound in Great Britain by Ashford Colour Press, Gosport, Hampshire.

The publishers' policy is to use paper manufactured from sustainable forests.

Contents

Introduction	1
Why publish on the Web?	1
Organisation of this book	2
The Web site for this book	3
Special icons	4
1 ■ Getting to grips with FrontPage	5
Getting started	6
Launching FrontPage	6
Shortcut icon	6
Quitting FrontPage	7
Exploring FrontPage	7
Screen	7
Title bar	8
System buttons	8
ScreenTips	9
Using the mouse	9
Pointing and using the left mouse button	9
The right mouse button or the context menus	10
Menu bar	11
Dialog boxes	12
Main toolbars	13
Other toolbars	15
Status bar	16
Navigating between views	17
Views bar	17

FrontPage 2000

2 ■ Web, HTML and Help — 19

- What is FrontPage for? — 20
- Web principles — 20
- HTML — 20
  - Visualisation of the HTML format — 24
- FrontPage, HTML editor — 25
  - WYSIWYG — 26
- HTML lovers, Microsoft is your friend! — 26
  - Protected code source — 26
  - Working with existing HTML code — 27
  - HTML code formatting — 27
  - Colours for the HTML code — 28
- Help! — 29
  - Help from the Contents — 29
  - Answers Wizard — 31
  - Help Index — 32
  - The What's This? command — 33

3 ■ Sites: creating and organising — 35

- The concept of a site — 36
  - The site you are going to produce — 36
  - Choosing the subject — 36
- Site creation — 37
  - Creation of a one-page site — 38
  - Creation of a site with a template or a Wizard — 39
  - Creation of a site from a folder — 41
  - Importing a site — 42
- Site management — 43
  - Assigning a name to a site — 43
  - Closing a site — 44
  - Opening an existing site — 44
  - Deleting a site — 45
- Site settings — 47
  - Language — 47
  - Choice of the script language — 47

Contents

Customising the navigation bar settings	48
Folder management	49
What is the Private folder for?	49
Folder creation	50
Deletion of folders	50
Renaming a folder	50

4 ■ Pages: how to create and organise them — 51

The page concept	52
Start Page	52
Folders view	53
Page creation and management	53
Insertion of fresh pages	53
Opening a page	56
Naming a page	57
Deleting a page	58
Saving a page	58
Closing a page	58
Print Preview	59
Formatting before printing	59
Printing a page	60
Viewing in the browser	61
Page organisation	62
Placing pages in a folder	62
Page settings	63
Defining spell checking	63
Defining the target browser	64
Automatic page creation	65
Creating pages with a template	65
Style Sheets	66

5 ■ Text — 69

Page view	70
Entering text	70

Non-printable characters	71
Forced hyphenation and accented uppercase characters	72
Text in the start page	72
Inserting a blank line	74
Moving within the text	74
Moving quickly within the text	75
Inserting files	76
Creating a text file	76
Selecting text	80
Editing text	81
Undo/Redo an action	81
Other pages in your site	82

6 ■ Text: formatting — 85

Formatting procedures	86
Formatting characters	86
Defining fonts by default	86
Font modification	87
Modification of the font size	88
Changing case	89
Adding colour to the text	90
Defining a customised colour	90
The Font dialog box	92
Formatting paragraphs	93
Modification of alignment	93
Creation and modification of indents	94
Paragraph dialog box	95
Bulleted and numbered lists	96
Modifying bullets and numbers	97
Borders and Shading	98
Applying a border to a paragraph	98
Paragraph shading	99
Format painting	101

Contents

7 ■ Pictures: inserting and formatting — 103

- Inserting pictures — 104
  - Clip Art images — 104
  - Finding a Clip Art image — 106
  - Establishing a picture library — 107
  - Inserting a picture file — 108
  - Saving images — 109
  - Saving extensions — 110
  - Deleting images — 110
- Web images — 110
  - Retrieving pictures on the Web — 111
- Formatting images — 111
  - Resizing an image — 111
  - Placing an image in relation to the text — 112
  - Creating a thumbnail — 114
  - Inserting text into a picture — 116
  - Pictures Toolbar — 116
  - Site continuity — 118

8 ■ Advanced formatting and Help tools — 119

- Themes — 120
- Formatting pages — 121
  - Framing all text in a page — 121
  - Page background — 122
  - Coloured background — 123
  - Apply the background from another page — 125
  - Creating a picture background — 126
  - Splitting paragraphs — 127
  - Inserting lines — 127
  - Modifying a line — 128
  - Copying a line — 128
- Text animation — 129
- Finding and replacing text — 130
- Spelling — 131

FrontPage 2000

AutoSpelling	131
Launching the Spell Checker	132

9 ■ Frames, tables and multimedia — 135

Frames	136
Frames Pages	137
Creating Frames Pages	137
Creating the first frame	139
Using an existing page	139
Creating the second frame	140
Defining the properties for created pages	140
Defining Frames properties	141
Defining Frames Pages	142
Saving Frames Pages	143
Testing Frames Pages	144
Tables	144
Creating a table	144
Entering text in a table	146
Borders	147
Modifying tables	149
Sound	149
Inserting sound	149
Video clips	151
Animated pictures	152
Modifying an animated GIF	152

10 ■ Forms and hyperlinks — 153

Forms	154
Creating a form	155
Fields	155
Main fields in forms	155
Inserting fields	156
Inserting a text box	157
Defining properties for a text box	157

Contents

Inserting a Scrolling Text Box	159
Inserting an option check box field	159
Defining Properties check box	160
Inserting multiple-choice check boxes	161
Inserting a drop-down menu field	161
Defining Properties for a drop-down menu field	161
Defining the Properties of Command buttons	162
Data processing	164
Hyperlinks	164
Creating hyperlinks to take you to other pages	165
Creating a picture which interacts with another page	166
Creating a hyperlink in the same page	166
Creating hyperlinks to another site	167
Deleting a hyperlink	167

11 ■ Site management — 169

Managing hyperlinks	170
Defining links colour	170
Checking links	171
Repairing broken links	173
Viewing all hyperlinks	174
Testing in the browser	174
Organising pages and pictures	175
Importing pages	175
Organising pictures	176
Site summary	177
Identifying slow-loading pages	178
Sorting files	178
Site structure	179
Defining the structure	179
Managing pages in the Navigation view	180

Printing the site structure	181
Modifying your site	181
Work organisation	181

12 ■ Publishing and security 185

IP	186
Connections	187
Publishing your site	190
Publishing with FrontPage extensions	190
Publishing without FrontPage extensions	191
Servers	192
FrontPage personal Web server	193
Microsoft personal Web server	193
Installing and uninstalling a server	193
Configuring the Administrator	196
Server Properties	197
The General tab of the Server Properties dialog box	198
The Startup tab of the Server Properties dialog box	198
The Administration tab of the Server Properties dialog box	199
The Services tab of the Server Properties dialog box	199
Securing your server	200
Testing the Web server	201
Visiting your site	202

Index 207

Introduction

FrontPage 2000 is an HTML editor, i.e. a way of processing text to create Web sites without having to write HTML code. You do not need to be a computer wizard to create a site, or to know the Web tag-based language. FrontPage 2000 generates HTML in accordance with your instructions, your page formatting options, your insertions of pictures, sound, animation, and so on. And the beauty of it is that even HTML programmers can use FrontPage, because it is also meant to be used in this way.

FrontPage 2000 also offers several other features, such as site management, hyperlinks verification and folders organisation.

This software is the perfect tool for publishing on the Web, with the best possible level of quality and creativity.

■ Why publish on the Web?

This book is aimed at all those who wish to publish a site on the Web and who want to be able to do it without delay. One of the services offered by the Internet, the World Wide Web, is an extraordinary communication medium, and this is not just a passing fad: the Web will become indispensable. It offers some considerable advantages: economy, speed, simplicity and universality. To be on the Web is to be up to date with our times.

Before reading this book, think about the site that you would like to publish. Here are some golden rules to take into account when you want to publish on the Web: deal with one theme or a subject at a time, develop a plan or a flow chart for the design of your pages (title, subject, end or conclusion) and keep within the law (no racism, pornography, or neo-nazi theories or other unmentionables, such as paedophile literature).

■ Organisation of this book

The two first chapters are aimed at the complete novice: here you will discover the different elements of FrontPage 2000 and their function. The two principal functions of FrontPage 2000 are creation of Web pages and organisation of a Web site (formerly known as Explorer and Editor).

We have chosen a theme: the Impressionist painters. The ideal would be to follow scrupulously the stages of the creation of the pages of the site and to carry out all the operations indicated. When completed, your creation can be your model for your future work.

- **Chapter 1** shows you the procedures for opening and closing FrontPage and the various elements of the interface, and explains the new Menu Bar and Toolbars features. You will also get to know the FrontPage Views.
- **Chapter 2** explains the Web, the HTML language and the WYSIWYG principle. In this chapter, HTML users will discover all the new features for creating and modifying HTML code. You will also learn how to work with FrontPage Help tools.
- **Chapter 3** describes the creation and organisation of a site structure. These notions will be dealt with in more detail in Chapter 11.
- **Chapter 4** describes the procedures for creating pages, how to organise them, how to open them, and so on.
- **Chapter 5** introduces a number of different procedures for inserting text.

Introduction

- **Chapter 6** teaches you how to format text.
- **Chapter 7** explains the insertion and formatting of pictures.
- **Chapter 8** describes advanced format functions as well as the definition of page properties.
- **Chapter 9** shows you how to create tables and frames and how to insert multimedia elements.
- **Chapter 10** explains how to create forms, how to insert fields and how to handle data.
- **Chapter 11** shows you best practice for site management.
- **Chapter 12** explains how to publish a site on the Internet and on an Intranet.

■ The Web site for this book

To view the site created for this title, go to Pearson Professional Education Web site at **http://computing.business-minds.com/frontpage**. You can even download the entire contents of the site in order to install it on your hard disk and browse it off line, i.e. without being connected to the Internet.

1. Connect to the Pearson Professional Education Web site at **http://computing.business-minds.com/frontpage**.
2. Click on the 'Download the zipped file' link at the top right of the home page.
3. The 'File Download' dialog box will now appear. Select 'save this file to disk' and click on OK.
4. Choose a folder on your hard drive in which to save painters.zip and then click on 'save' in order to start downloading the site.
5. Once the download is complete click on OK. You can now close your Web browser.

FrontPage 2000

6. Having completed the downloading, decompress the file with the help of compression software such as WinZip. The following instructions are for WinZip users. For more information about compressing data, please refer to *A Simple Guide to Winzip and PKZip* (2000) also published in this series.
7. In Windows NT Explorer open painters.zip. Select all the files, ensure that 'Use folder names' is checked and click on Extract.
8. You will be asked where you want to save the unzipped files. Create a folder called **painters** and then click OK.
9. When the files have been unzipped, open the **painters** folder and double click on the **summary.htm** file to open the home page in your browser.
10. And now, enjoy navigating the site dedicated to the Impressionist painters off line.

■ Special icons

Next to some text and figures, you will find some icons which underline important points.

This symbol provides you with suggestions and tips: keyboard shortcuts, advanced techniques, and so on.

Here you will find additional information.

This symbol warns you about problems you may encounter. It also warns you what not to do. If you follow the instructions, you should not have any problems.

This icon shown on the margins of paragraphs signals the procedures necessary to create the Impressionist site.

This icon shown on the margins of paragraphs indicates new features of FrontPage 2000.

1
Getting to grips with FrontPage

Getting started
Exploring FrontPage
Navigating between views

Throughout this chapter, you will learn how to launch and quit the software. You will then be introduced to the elements of its environment as well as the new features of its interface.

■ Getting started

To start with, you should get acquainted with the procedures for launching and closing FrontPage.

Launching FrontPage

To launch FrontPage, click on **Start, Programs, Microsoft FrontPage**. You may also click on the **Microsoft FrontPage** icon in the **Office** toolbar.

> *If the Office toolbar is not displayed, click on Start, Programs, Microsoft Office Tools, Microsoft Office Shortcut bar.*

Shortcut icon

If you find the **Office** toolbar bar somewhat cluttered, but still wish to launch FrontPage rapidly, you can quite easily create a shortcut icon. This will be displayed on your Desktop for you just to double click to launch the software.

To create a shortcut icon:

1. Click on **Start, Programs**.
2. In the drop down menu, right click on **Microsoft FrontPage**, then, still holding down the mouse button, drag on the Desktop.
3. When you release the button, a context menu is displayed (see Figure 1.1). Click on **Create shortcut(s) here**.

The icon is now placed on the Desktop.

1: Getting to grips with FrontPage

Figure 1.1 You can create a shortcut icon to launch FrontPage quickly.

Quitting FrontPage

To close FrontPage, several procedures are available:

- Click on **File, Quit**.
- Click on the **Close** button (which is represented by an X) in the title bar.
- Press the **Alt+F4** keyboard keys.
- Click on the system check box (represented by the FrontPage sign) in the Title bar. Select **Close** from the context menu.

■ Exploring FrontPage

Now that you know how to launch and quit FrontPage, let us discover the screen, the different elements of the environment and its new features. In version 2000, they have gone out of their way to make your life easier.

Screen

The screen displays the different elements required to navigate between the various folders and to activate the commands (see Figure 1.2). Unlike version 98 which contained two views, Editor and Explorer, all the views are now grouped into one.

The following sections describe the various bars and their functions.

FrontPage 2000

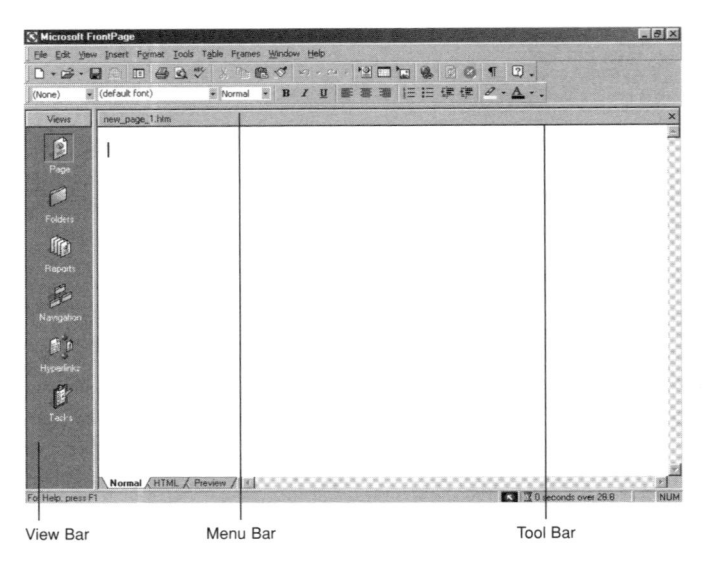

Figure 1.2 The FrontPage screen.

(View Bar, Menu Bar, Tool Bar)

Title bar

The Title bar (see Figure 1.3) displays the name of the program. When you begin to create a site, the Title bar will display the name that you have given it. The system buttons are located to the extreme right.

Figure1.3 The FrontPage title bar.

System buttons

The system buttons are a common feature of all applications running under Windows 95 and Windows 98. They let you close, maximise, restore or minimise the active window.

Here are the different functions of the system buttons:

1: Getting to grips with FrontPage

× Enlarges the window to its maximum size.

▫ Reduces the window to a small icon in the Task bar.

▫ When you are in full screen, reduces the window by half.

▫ Closes FrontPage.

ScreenTips

FrontPage can show you brief information on buttons, commands and options very quickly. These are the ScreenTips.

To display the ScreenTip for an icon, place your pointer on the relevant icon, leave it there for a moment and the ScreenTip will appear.

To display the ScreenTip for a dialog box option, click on the question mark, then place your pointer on the relevant option.

> *If the ScreenTip is not displayed, click on **Tools**, **Customize**, then on the **Options** tab. Activate the **Show ScreenTips** option. Click on **Close** to confirm.*

Using the mouse

The mouse is indispensable in the Windows environment. The right mouse button opens a shortcut menu. On the screen, the mouse is represented by an oblique white arrow, called a 'pointer'. This pointer changes shape depending on the task performed.

When you move the mouse, the pointer reproduces its moves on the screen.

Pointing and using the left mouse button

- **Pointing.** Placing the tip of the mouse arrow onto an object on the screen.
- **Clicking.** Pressing once on the left mouse button after having pointed to an object.

FrontPage 2000

- **Double-clicking.** Clicking twice quickly with the left mouse button.
- **Dragging.** Clicking on an object and, holding down the button, moving the object along the screen.

The right mouse button or the context menus

The actions which can be carried out on an object are grouped in a menu known as 'context'. It is called a context menu because its contents is linked to whatever object was located where the menu was opened. Throughout this book, we will give priority to context menus procedures.

- **Right click.** Having selected an object with the mouse, click the right mouse button to display the corresponding context menu (see Figure 1.4).

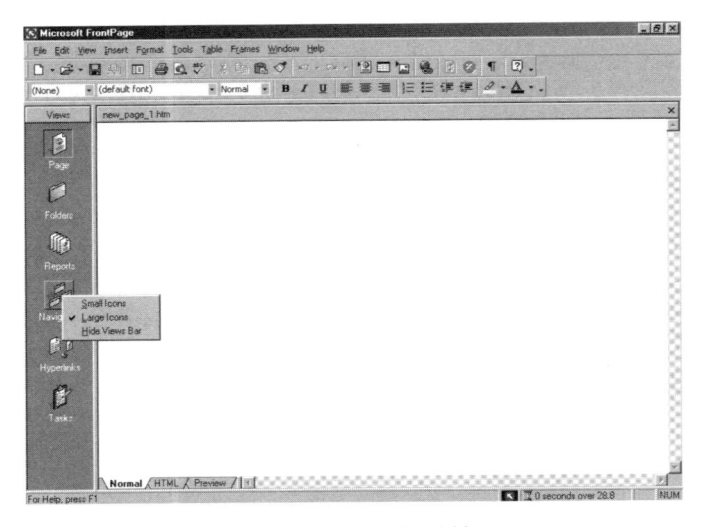

Figure 1.4 The context menu of the Navigation folder.

Menu bar

The Menu bar (see Figure 1.5) is located underneath the Title bar. Each menu (File, View, and so on) opens a drop-down list which offers a number of commands. The menus follow several conventions:

- The grey commands are not available, the commands in black are available.
- An arrowpoint next to a command indicates that you can open a submenu containing other commands.
- An ellipsis (three dots) after a command indicates that it offers a dialog box for selecting various options, defining various choices, and so on.
- An icon in front of a command indicates that it is recommended as a shortcut in one of the toolbars.
- The combination of keyboard keys such as **Ctrl** and **Alt** followed by a letter displayed next to a command means that command can be implemented with a keyboard shortcut. Pressing these keyboard keys automatically executes the command or opens the corresponding dialog box (for example, by pressing the *Ctrl+P* keyboard keys, you will open the Print dialog box).

File Edit View Insert Format Tools Table Frames Window Help

Figure 1.5 The FrontPage Menu bar.

In order to make your task easier, version 2000 allows automatic customisation of menus. Therefore, as you work, menus become tailor-made to your choices and only display the commands you are using. To view all the menu options, simply click on the two arrowheads, at the end of the menu, or double-click on the menu name (for example, double-click on **File** to view the default menu).

FrontPage 2000

If this option is not activated or if, on the other hand, you wish to deactivate it, you must specify your choice in the Customize dialog box.

To modify custom menu options:

1. Right click on the Menu bar and select **Customize**.
2. Click on the **Options** tab (see Figure 1.6). Activate and deactivate options according to your needs. Click on **Close** to confirm.

Figure 1.6 The Customize dialog box lets you define Menu bar options.

Dialog boxes

We have seen that the commands followed by three dots open a dialog box where you can define choices, activate options, and so on. Other commands also open dialog boxes.

In the 2000 version, the Open (see Figure 1.7) and Save dialog boxes now have a button bar at the side exactly like the one in Outlook. This provides rapid access to the most often used folders and documents. The dialog boxes are now larger so they are easier to work with.

1: Getting to grips with FrontPage

Figure 1.7 FrontPage Open File dialog box.

The button represented by a left-pointing arrow has the same function as in the Internet browsers: it lets you return to the previous selection.

Main toolbars

Positioned underneath the Menu Bar, toolbars provide quick access to a number of standard commands. As the default, FrontPage displays two toolbars: Standard and Format, but you can also display others.

To display a toolbar, right click anywhere on a toolbar, then click on the bar to be displayed (see Figure 1.8).

To hide a toolbar, right click on a toolbar and click on the one you wish to hide.

Previously fixed and perhaps too dominant, the toolbars are now 'à la carte': they take up minimum space on the screen as they are displayed next to each other, and they change according to your needs. To view other icons on a toolbar, simply click on the two right-pointing arrowheads at the end of the bar on the right.

Figure 1.8 Quick display of a toolbar.

The Customize toolbars options are now very simple.

To customise a toolbar, after it is displayed on the screen:

1. Right click on the toolbar and select **Customize**.
2. In the **Customize** dialog box, the **Options** tab lets you define precisely the display (**Large icons**, **List font names** in their font, **Show ScreenTips**, and so on), the **Toolbars** tab allows you to activate a toolbar and create a new one, while the **Commands** tab lists the various categories of buttons as well as their icons.
3. To add an icon to a toolbar, select the category in the **Commands** tab, click on the button to be added from the list on the right and drag it to the relevant toolbar. Click on **Close** to confirm.

To remove a button, click the arrowheads in the relevant toolbar, select **Add or Remove Buttons** (see Figure 1.9) and click on the option check box next to the command to be removed.

1: Getting to grips with FrontPage

Figure 1.9 Quick removal of a button in a toolbar.

Other toolbars

FrontPage offers several additional toolbars which you can access with the same procedures explained previously.

The following additional toolbars are available:

- **Tables.** Lets you insert a table, columns, remove cells, and so on.
- **Pictures.** Lets you insert rectangles, shapes, rotate an image, and so on.
- **Reporting.** Lets you create a summary for the site quickly, display all the files, view previous files, and so on.
- **DHTML Effects.** Lets you add animation effects to the images and/or to the text.
- **Navigation.** Lets you modify the zoom, the page orientation and the site structure.
- **Positioning.** Lets you position text, images, and so on.

FrontPage 2000

- **Style.** Lets you create, modify or remove the style of a page. A style is a set of formats (alignment, spacing, appearance, and so on).

Each toolbar will be described in detail in the following chapters.

Status bar

Located at the bottom of the screen (see Figure 1.10), the status bar displays information on the work carried out.

| For Help, press F1 | 0 seconds over 28.8 | NUM |

Figure 1.10 FrontPage status bar.

If the status bar is not displayed, you must activate it:

1. Click on **Tools, Options**.
2. In the dialog box, click on the **General** tab (see Figure 1.11). Click on the option **Show status bar** to activate it, then on **OK** to confirm.

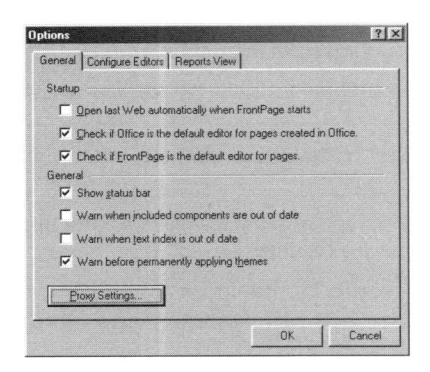

Figure 1.11 Displaying the status bar.

1: Getting to grips with FrontPage

■ Navigating between views

As we have already seen, the views previously grouped in Explorer and Editor are now together in the Views bar. We are now going to learn how to move between the various views in FrontPage. In the following chapters, we will see how to use the various views.

Views bar

Located to the left of the screen (see Figure 1.12), the Views bar lets you navigate quickly between the various views.

Figure 1.12 The Views Bar lets you switch between different modes.

This is the list of the various views and their functions:

Page. Where you do most of your content creation and editing for your Web pages. The Page view allows you to control the final appearance of the page, because it shows all the elements while you enter them (text, pictures, tables, form fields and others).

FrontPage 2000

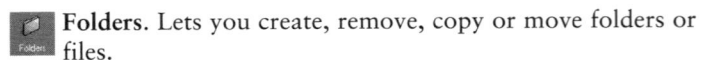

Folders. Lets you create, remove, copy or move folders or files.

Reports. Shows you a complete list of all files in the current Web structure, along with information about each file. No folders are shown. Management information from Reports view can help you discover and fix problems with your structure (overloaded pages, unused files, and so on).

Navigation. Allows you to organise, display, print and modify the hierarchical structure of your site.

Hyperlinks. Displays the connection – hyperlinks – between your pages or with other sites.

Tasks. When a site is produced by several authors, this view allows you to manage tasks, assignments and priorities.

To move between views, click on the corresponding icon in the **Views** bar.

To hide the Views bar, click on **View, Views bar**.

To display the Views bar, click on **View, Views bar**.

2 Web, HTML and Help

- What is FrontPage for?
- Web principles
- HTML
- FrontPage, HTML editor
- HTML lovers, Microsoft is your friend!
- Help!

FrontPage 2000

You are now going to be introduced to the Web. You will discover how it works and you will become acquainted with the HTML format (*HyperText Markup Language*). To complete the task, you will learn everything there is to know about getting help while you work.

■ What is FrontPage for?

FrontPage is a program for creating and managing Web sites. For this purpose, it provides you with all the tools required for the conception and creation of a site. These are the various tools that you will study in the following chapters, together with the way they work. At the end of this chapter, you will be shown how to use the various Help functions in FrontPage.

Of course, you are in a rush to start building your first site, but you must read the various instructions in this chapter before you can start working.

■ Web principles

The Web (World Wide Web) is one of the Internet services, without doubt the most widely-used one together with e-mail. It offers a vast amount of information on scientific matters as well as on the world of cinema, sport, news, literature, and so on. Through a hyperlinks system (see Figure 2.1), you can navigate between pages and between sites. The documents on show may be texts, pictures, charts, sounds, and so on.

> *Hypertext is a word, or a group of words, shown in colour, at times underlined, in a Web page. This lets you access another page or another site. When you point to a hypertext link, the pointer becomes a hand.*

2: Web, HTML and Help

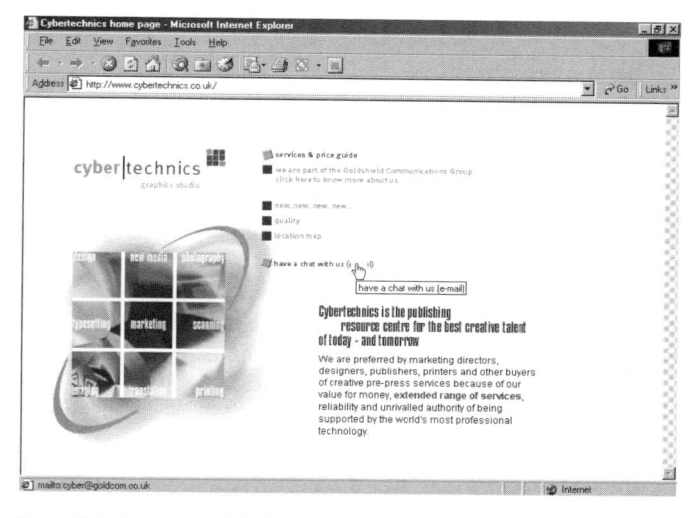

Figure 2.1 A hyperlink is indicated by a hand in the browser.

A Web page is a file, or a document, containing information (text, sound or video) which is displayed in the browser window when you 'surf' the Web.

A site is a set of pages, pictures and documents.

■ HTML

When the principle of the Internet was established, professionals asked themselves how they were going to share data from a computer network with users worldwide. The solution was the creation of a system which allows data to be marked up with special codes: tags. These tags indicate how specific data should be presented to the document reader. Therefore, when an Internet surfer goes on-line and navigates within a site, the tags specify to the browser how the page should be viewed (bold, italic, uppercase, colours, and so on).

FrontPage 2000

To demonstrate this, let us take a example. Here is some text:

THE IMPRESSIONISTS
Masters of colour, inveterate dreamers, they have been scattered across our museums and a few lucky art collectors. Thanks to *Manet, Monet, Morisot, Sisley, Cézanne, Van Gogh, and so on.*

The tag language specifies the format for the various parts of the data. In our example, the title is in uppercase, Times New Roman, 10-point, bold; the text is in the same font, but in lower case, with part of it in italic. The tags mark individual bits of data to specify how these must be displayed. This is what the above text looks like in tag language:

```
<p><font face= Times New Roman"><b">THE IMPRESSIONISTS
</b></font></p>

<p><font face="Times New Roman"> Masters of colour,
inveterate dreamers, they have been scattered across
our museums and a few lucky art collectors. Thanks to
<i>Manet</i>, <i>Monet</i>, <i>Morisot</i>,
<i>Sisley</i>, <i>Cézanne</i>, <i>Van Gogh</i>, and so
on/ </font></p>
```

Figure 2.2 This is what the above text looks like on screen.

In the example, we had to use four tags: `<b>` marks the bold attribute, `<p>` marks a paragraph, `<i>` marks the italic attribute and `<font face="Times New Roman">` indicates the typeface.

2: Web, HTML and Help

```
new_page_1.htm
<html>

<head>
<meta http-equiv="Content-Language" content="en-gb">
<meta http-equiv="Content-Type" content="text/html; charset=windows-1252">
<meta name="GENERATOR" content="Microsoft FrontPage 4.0">
<meta name="ProgId" content="FrontPage.Editor.Document">
<title>New Page 1</title>
</head>

<body>

<p style="line-height: 100%; margin-top: 0" align="left"><font face="Times New Roman" size="2"><b>THE
IMPRESSIONISTS</b></font></p>
<p style="line-height: 100%; margin-top: 0" align="left"><font face="Times New Roman"><font size="2">
of colour, inveterate dreamers, they have been scattered across our museums and
a few lucky art collectors. Thanks to <i>Manet</i>, <i>Monet</i>, <i>Morisot</i>,
<i>Sisley</i>, <i>Cézanne</i>, <i>Van Gogh</i>, etc</font>.</font></p>

</body>

</html>
```

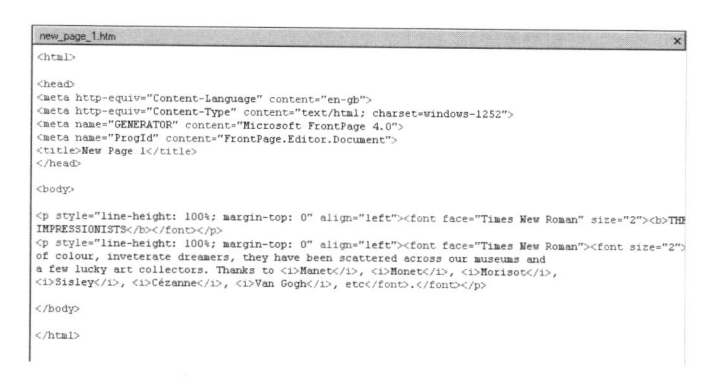

Figure 2.3 The HTML code in the example, viewed in a browser.

The surfer who will read your page, using a browser, will see Figure 2.3.

The browser is the tool which lets you view a Web document. It is the browser which translates the tag language. This is a simple comparison: to listen to an audio cassette, you need a tape recorder. The browser is the Web tape recorder.

This tagging technique is called HTML (*HyperText Markup Language*). Once this language became known, computer users throughout the world started to prepare data in this format, which allowed them to share data with anybody who connected to their server. The Web was born.

With time, an increasing number of tags was created and it soon become impossible to remember them all by heart. Designers carried on writing their Web pages with a simple text editor, but they were tearing their hair out at the prospect of the vast number of tags they had to use. Creating one page containing text, pictures and sound in HTML format could take several days.

FrontPage 2000

Visualisation of the HTML format

If you wish, you can view the page that you have just created in HTML format.

To display the HTML format, click on the **HTML** tab, at the bottom of the screen (see Figure 2.4).

```
<html>
<head>
<title>Cybertechnics home page</title>
<meta http-equiv="Content-Type" content="text/html; charset=iso-8859-1">
</head>

<body bgcolor="#FFFFFF" background="images/mainBack.gif">
<table width="620" border="0" cellspacing="0" cellpadding="0">
  <tr>
    <td width="50"><img src="images/transPix.gif" width="50" height="1"></td>
    <td width="63"><img src="images/transPix.gif" width="63" height="1"></td>
    <td width="64"><img src="images/transPix.gif" width="64" height="1"></td>
    <td width="59"><img src="images/transPix.gif" width="59" height="1"></td>
    <td width="29"><img src="images/transPix.gif" width="29" height="1"></td>
    <td width="14"><img src="images/transPix.gif" width="14" height="1"></td>
    <td width="72"><img src="images/transPix.gif" width="72" height="1"></td>
    <td width="269"><img src="images/transPix.gif" width="269" height="1"></td>
  </tr>
  <tr>
    <td colspan="4"></td>
    <td><img src="images/transPix.gif" width="1" height="45"></td>
    <td rowspan="9"></td>
    <td colspan="2"></td>
  </tr>
  <tr valign="top">
    <td colspan="4" align="right"><img src="images/cyberLogo.gif" width="186" height="54"></td>
    <td></td>
    <td colspan="2"><img src="images/buttons1.gif" width="256" height="43" border="0" usemap="#Hom
  </tr>
  <tr>
    <td colspan="4"></td>
```

Figure 2.4 A site and its tag language. HTML.

2: Web, HTML and Help

If you are not too fond of using tabs, you can view the HTML code in the default Normal view.

To view the HTML in Normal view, click on **View, Reveal Tags**. You can also press the keyboard keys **CTRL+/** (see Figure 2.5).

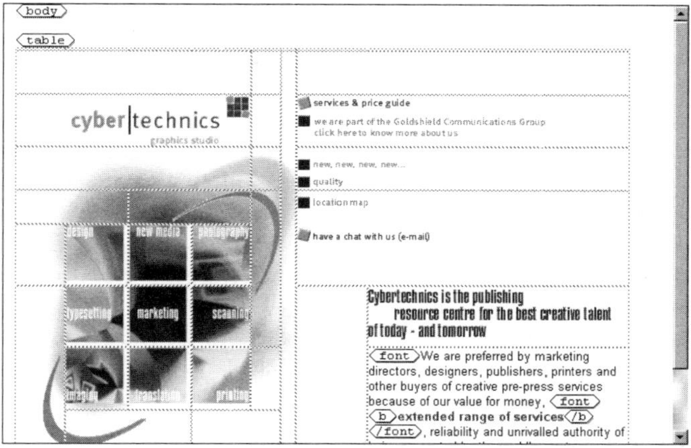

Figure 2.5 You can view the HTML code in Normal view.

To hide the HTML in Normal view, click on **View, Reveal Tags**. You can also press the **CTRL+/** keyboard keys.

■ FrontPage, HTML editor

We have just seen how formats are defined for the Web. For years a knowledge of HTML had become a must to be able to publish on the Web, which limited the number of users. But times change, you will be shown in the following chapters how, nowadays, with FrontPage, anybody can create Web pages quickly.

WYSIWYG

In the years following the birth of HTML language, a new, more user-friendly approach has developed: the WYSIWYG concept. This acronym, which applies to word-processing programs or DTP, means '*What You See Is What You Get*', in other words 'what you enter on your screen is what you will get in your final document'.

Away with tags and coding! With a WYSIWYG program such as FrontPage, you simply enter the text, then format it, as you would in any word-processing application. Do not be fooled, dear old HTML is still there and will be around for a long while. But it stays in the background, 'under the bonnet' of FrontPage. Every time you write and format text, FrontPage translates it to HTML format. In practice, HTML is still very much the format for writing Web pages, because browsers can only read this format. But you no longer need to encode the tags yourself: FrontPage will do it for you!

■ HTML lovers, Microsoft is your friend!

It is true that in the previous version of FrontPage it was already possible to modify HTML tags, but these functions have been incredibly enhanced in the 2000 version. New working methods allow all programmers who work in a text editor and who know HTML perfectly to generate code much more quickly with FrontPage. The door is now open to all developers who wish to maintain their coding and formatting practice and for those who wish to navigate between several HTML editors.

Protected source code

Let us imagine that you have created a text, with its lines of code in any HTML editor and that you want to modify this code in FrontPage. The solution is to open the document in its editor, and integrate it in FrontPage. In previous versions, this type of manipulation had the nasty habit of modifying the language or the order of tags, but this does not happen in FrontPage 2000: the document is imported without any modification whatsoever. There is nothing you need to do for this to work: this function is active as the default and cannot be removed.

Working with existing HTML code

If you want to insert or remove HTML code, simply go to HTML view (see the section on viewing HTML format), then follow the procedures you normally use in your HTML editor.

You can only modify your HTML code using the HTML view. Viewing the HTML code in the Normal mode does not allow you to carry out modifications.

HTML code formatting

Microsoft has taken into account a basic concept: freedom of choice for the user. You can therefore define precisely the HTML code formats that you wish to insert into a page. Your working habits are safeguarded and you do not need to be slaves to the Microsoft rule.

To define the HTML code format:

1. Click on **Tools, Page Options**.
2. Click on the **HTML Source** tab (see Figure 2.6).
3. Activate and/or deactivate the options and define your choice. When you have made all your decisions, click on **OK** to confirm.

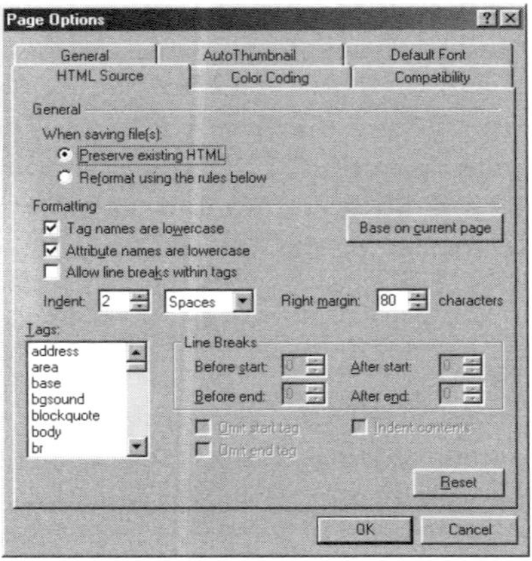

FrontPage 2000

Figure 2.6 Define the HTML code format.

Colours for the HTML code

If you do not like blue, which is the HTML code default colour in FrontPage, you can choose a brilliant yellow or a hot red for a better effect.

To modify the HTML code colour:

1. Click on **Tools, Page Options**.
2. Click on the **Colour Coding** tab (see Figure 2.7).
3. Activate and/or deactivate the options, define your choice. When you have finished, click on **OK** to confirm.

To reset the default display colour for the HTML code, click on **Tools, Page Options**, then on the **Colour Coding** tab. Click on the **Reset Colors** button, then on **OK** to confirm.

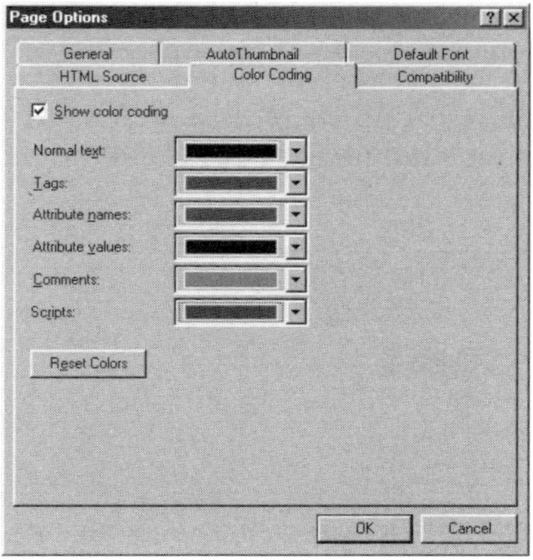

2: Web, HTML and Help

Figure 2.7 Define the HTML tags colours.

■ Help!

FrontPage offers several methods to get Help, accessible with the question mark in the Menu bar:

- **Microsoft FrontPage Help**. This command opens the FrontPage Help which has three tabs: Contents, Index and Answer Wizard. With these tabs, you can search a folder or a command in Help.
- **What's This**? This command lets you activate the context Help for a button, a command or a dialog box.

You can also connect to the Microsoft site to find out about the latest news, tips and upgrades.

To visit the Microsoft FrontPage site, click on the question mark, then select **Office on the Web**. You must, of course, be linked to the Internet. Once on the site, simply navigate and read the sections you are interested in.

FrontPage 2000

Help from the Contents

You can display Help sections from the Contents.

To open the Help Contents, click on **Help,** then on the question mark, which is **Microsoft FrontPage Help**. Click on the **Contents** tab (see Figure 2.8).

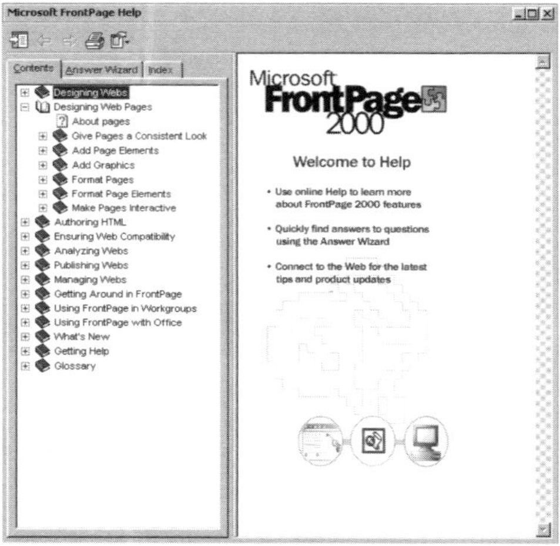

Figure 2.8 The Help Contents lets you browse the various Help topics.

This is what you should do to use Contents at its best:

- Each closed book offers a Help topic. Double-click on it to open it.
- Each open book shows the various sections of a topic. Double-click on it to close the topic.
- Each question mark offers a Help topic on a specific subject. Double-click on it to open it. Its contents are displayed in the area to the right (see Figure 2.9).

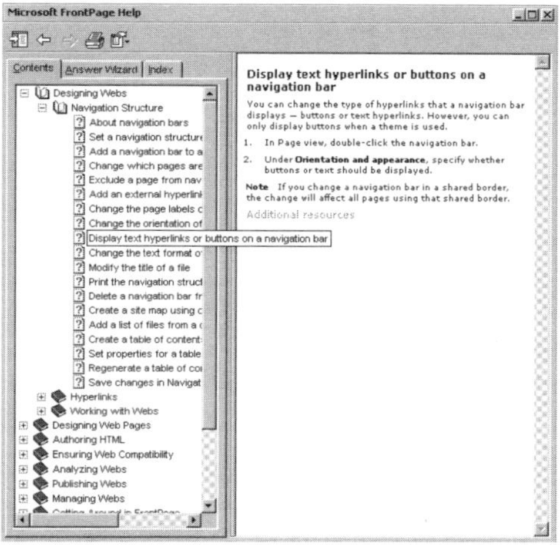

2: Web, HTML and Help

Figure 2.9 A Help topic is indicated by a question mark. Its contents are displayed in the area to the right.

> *To print a Help topic, after display, click on the Print icon in the toolbar of the Help contents. Careful, do not forget to switch your printer on!*

The HTML Help concept, new in FrontPage 2000, allows you to work while you have Help on screen. If you wish to remove it from your screen, you will need to close it.

Answers Wizard

Answers Wizard allows you to ask questions to FrontPage in standard language.

To ask Help a question:

1. Click on **Help**, then select **Microsoft FrontPage Help**.
2. Click on the **Answers Wizard** tab (see Figure 2.10).

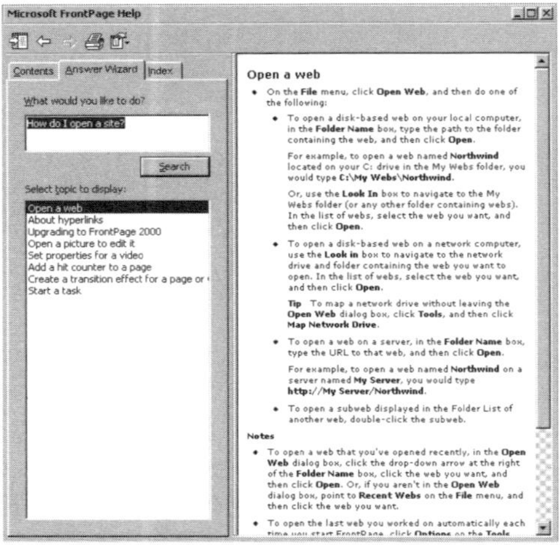

FrontPage 2000

Figure 2.10 The new Help function lets you ask a question directly in standard language.

In the text box of the **What would you like to do?** option, type your question. Click on the **Search** button or press the **Enter** key.

The answer is displayed in the **Select topic to display** option box.

3. Click on the topic which matches your question: this is displayed in the area on the right of the Help window.

Help Index

Index lets you carry out a quick search for a Help topic, because it narrows down the search area. You type a word and FrontPage opens a list of similar words. Then, you choose to display the topic which corresponds to the word or to the sentence which is closer to the one you want.

2: Web, HTML and Help

To use Index:

1. Click on the question mark and select **Microsoft FrontPage Help**.
2. Click on the **Index** tab. Enter the name of the topic you have been searching for in the **Type keywords** box (see Figure 2.11).

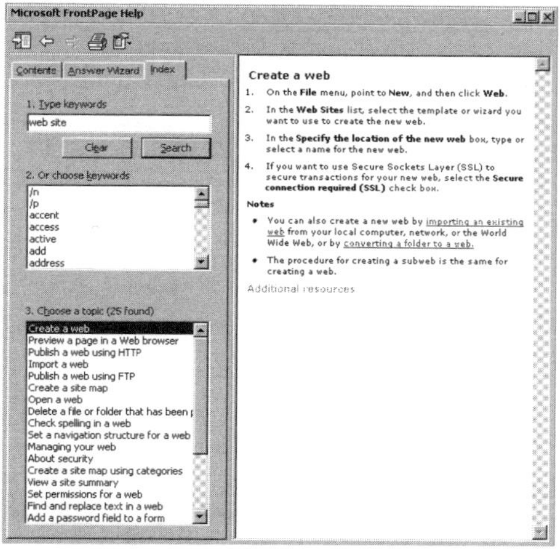

Figure 2.11 Enter the name of the topic you require or a word which describes the function you wish to find.

3. Several functions similar to the one you have chosen are displayed in the **Choose a topic** box (with the number of topics found). Click on the topic which matches your search: this is then displayed in the area to the right.

The What's This? command

Very practical, this command displays a balloon with the description of any element you have clicked on with this tool.

FrontPage 2000

To use the What's This? command:

1. Click on the question mark, then select **What's This?**

   The pointer becomes a question mark with a white arrow (see Figure 2.12).

Figure 2.12 The Pointer changes into a question mark with a black arrow when you select this command.

2. Click on the relevant command or button (see Figure 2.13).

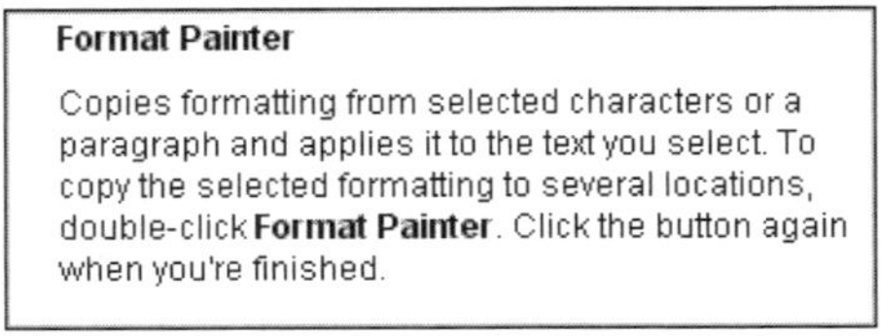

> **Format Painter**
>
> Copies formatting from selected characters or a paragraph and applies it to the text you select. To copy the selected formatting to several locations, double-click **Format Painter**. Click the button again when you're finished.

Figure 2.13 When you have clicked on the Format Painter button with the What's This? pointer, its description is displayed.

34

3 Sites: creating and organising

The concept of a site
Site creation
Site management
Site settings
Folder management

We are now going to examine the concept of a site, the insertion and removal of pages, and then you will learn how to define the structure of a site quickly. We will also give you some advice and rules for choosing a subject for your site.

■ The concept of a site

You have previously seen that a site is a set of pages, pictures, documents and other files. Of course, a site can also just have a single page.

The site you are going to produce

For a better understanding of FrontPage, we have chosen a single subject throughout the book. All the examples will refer to this site and its creation. We have already said that our site is based on the Impressionist movement, its origins, the various painters of this school, and so on. For a thorough understanding of the procedures involved, you should really create the site pages while you are studying this book. Obviously a number of the procedures explained in FrontPage are not directly related to the site. In order for you to execute only the commands which concern the creation of the site, the symbol at the beginning of this paragraph will be shown next to them.

Choosing the subject

It is pretty obvious that you are not going to publish the site that you will create while you are studying this book. It is therefore fundamental that you should understand from the start how important the choice of a subject is. Because the Web is the latest fad, a lot of people want to create their own site but it is totally useless to publish a site on the Web if you have nothing to say or to show. Unfortunately the Web is full of sites which have no interest for anybody. Try something different: show some imagination!

3: Sites: creating and organising

Of course, the problem of choosing a subject does not concern commercial companies which want to introduce their products: they know exactly what to say. Our advice here is only meant for people who wish to create their own personal site.

The first rule for a Web site is that you only introduce one subject at a time. Proposing several subjects in a site may bore the reader, who will quickly tire of it and just move away.

Here is a list of subjects which may give you some inspiration:

- your life, on condition that it is different, exciting;
- your talents;
- your interests, things you love;
- an association with which you work;
- your opinions, if your point of view sheds new light on a topic or a subject.

Some elementary rules:

- be attractive;
- be clear;
- be concise;
- be interesting;
- avoid cluttering;
- make sure that your pages look attractive.

■ Site creation

Now we are going to tackle all the concepts behind the creation of a site, either from a template, or from an existing folder or even a site created with another HTML editor.

FrontPage 2000

Creation of a one-page site

You are now going to create a site only containing a blank page, which will be the start page.

To create a new site:

1. Click on **File, New**.
2. In the drop-down menu, click on **Web** (see Figure 3.1). In the Options box, click on the arrow in the drop-down list and select the folder in which you want to place your site.

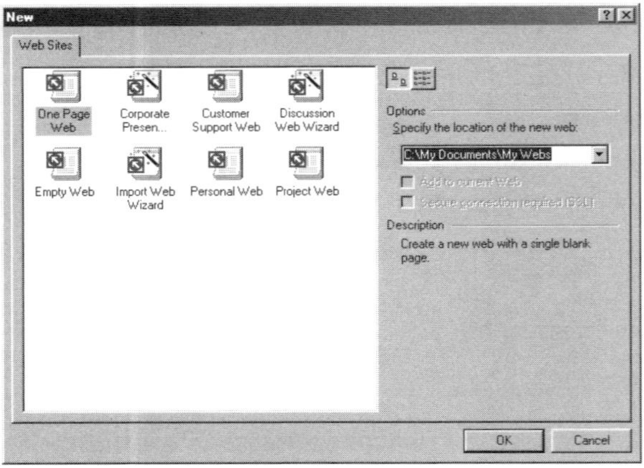

Figure 3.1 Creation of a blank site.

3. Click on the **One Page Web** icon, then on **OK** to confirm (see Figure 3.2).

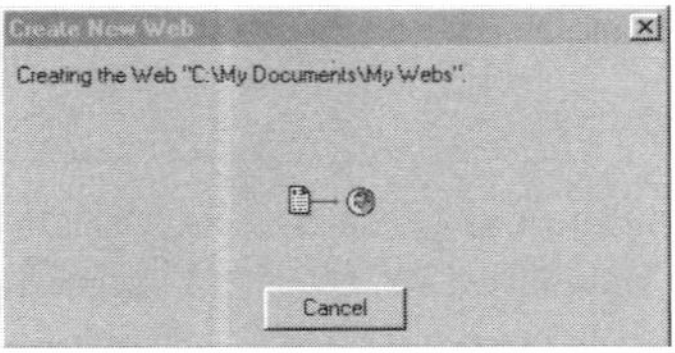

Figure 3.2 FrontPage creates the initial structure for your Web site.

3: Sites: creating and organising

*If you want to create a Web site without any page, click on the **Empty Web** icon in the New dialog box. Click on **OK** to confirm.*

Creation of a site with a template or a Wizard

FrontPage offers a number of site templates as well as Wizards that you can use to create a site quickly at your leisure. These templates are very practical if you are short of time.

To view the list of templates available for the creation of a site:

1. Click on **File, New**.
2. In the drop-down menu, click on **Web** (see Figure 3.1). The New dialog box is displayed. This shows the list of templates:

   - **Corporate Presence Wizard**. Allows you to create a Web site for your company quickly (see Figure 3.3). When you choose this Wizard, you will follow fifteen steps for defining your choices (choice of topic, identity information, the number of pages, and so on).

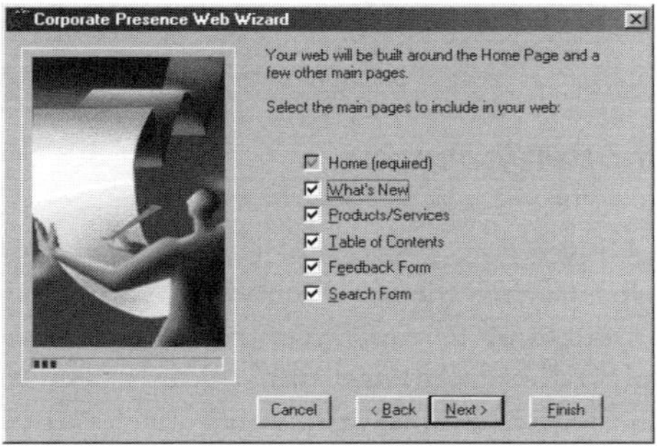

Figure 3.3 Corporate Presentation.

   - **Customer Support Web**. Allows you to create a site for a customer in a very little time. The example is based on

FrontPage 2000

the template of a software development company (see Figure 3.4). When you choose the template, this is displayed in FrontPage and you simply need to click in the various text boxes and enter the required text. You can also modify the settings for colour and background. To learn more about formatting procedures, refer to Chapter 5 and 6.

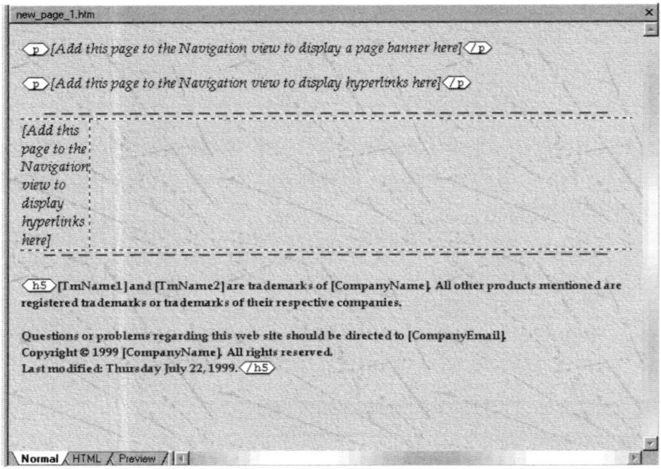

Figure 3.4 The Corporate Presentation template.

- **Project Web**. Allows you to create a site for a project containing a list of members, a schedule, status, an archive and discussion. If you have chosen this template, it is displayed in FrontPage and you only need to click in the defined text boxes and enter the required text. You can also modify the settings for colour and background.
- **Personal Web**. Allows you to create a site with pages on your interests, photos, favourite Web sites, and so on (see Figure 3.5).

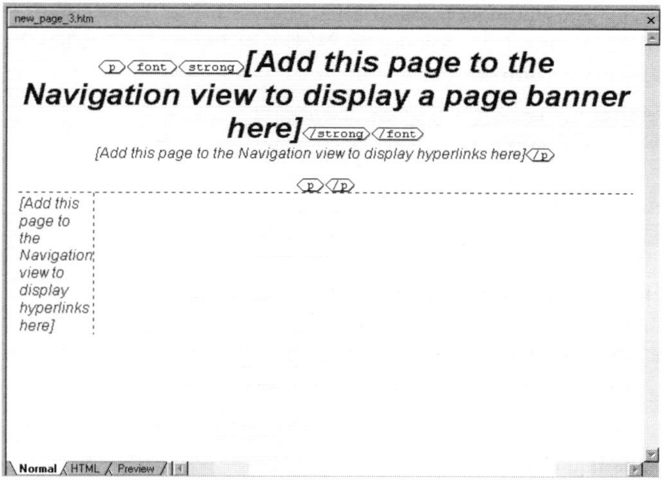

3: Sites: creating and organising

Figure 3.5 The Personal Web template.

If you have chosen this template, it is displayed in FrontPage and you only need to click in the defined text boxes and enter the required text. You can also modify the settings for colour and background.

Creation of a site from a folder

FrontPage lets you create a Web site from an existing folder. In practice, a folder in a site can be so large that sometimes it is better to allocate a whole site to it. This is how to proceed for this type of function.

You will be unable to convert the root folder in your hard disk by mistake.

To convert a folder to a Web site:

1. Open the site containing the folder to be converted. Click on the **View Folders** in the Views bar (see Chapter 1).

41

FrontPage 2000

2. In the **Folder List**, right click on the folder to be converted, then select **Convert to Web** (see Figure 3.6). Click on **Yes** to confirm.

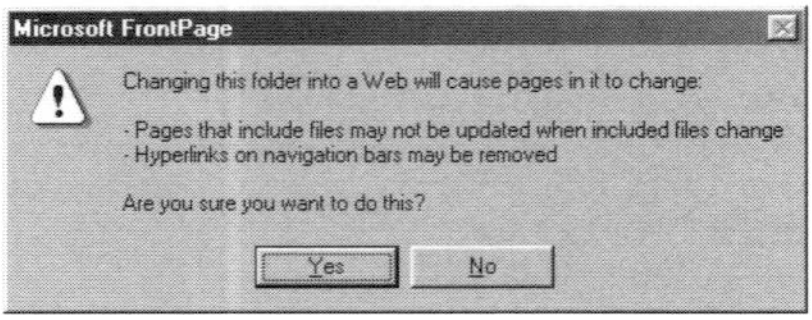

Figure 3.6 Confirm the conversion of the folder to site.

The site itself is not saved, but each modification is automatically saved by FrontPage and you need do nothing.

Importing a site

You can import an existing site created in another HTML editor or published on the Web.

To import a Web site:

1. Click on **File, Import** (see Figure 3.7).

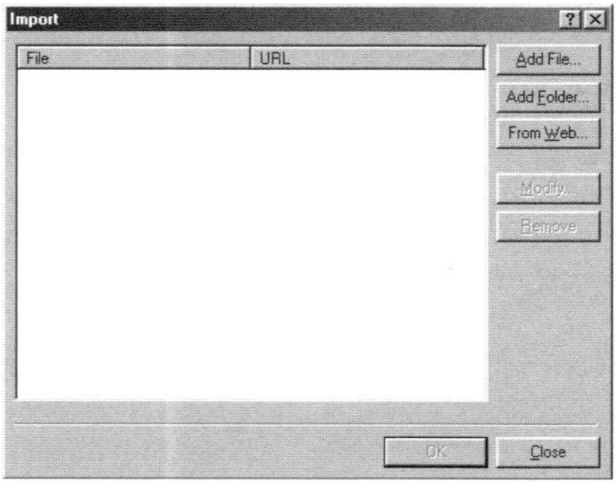

Figure 3.7 You can import a site which has been created in a different HTML editor.

3: Sites: creating and organising

2. Click on **Add File** or **Add Folder** to scan your hard disk. If you want to import a site published on the Web, click on **From Web**. The Import Web Wizard is displayed (see Figure 3.8). Follow the various steps. Click on **Finish**.

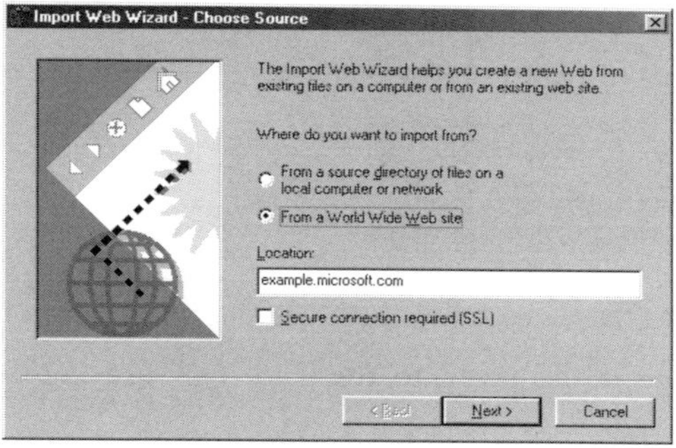

Figure 3.8 Use the Import Web Wizard to import a site published on the Web.

■ Site management

Let us see now how to name a site, what are the procedures for opening an existing site, how to remove it, and so on.

Assigning a name to a site

As the default, sites are called My Webs, followed by the number of their creation, which is not particularly clear. Let us therefore see how to name a site:

1. Click on **Tools, Web Settings**. Click on **General** (see Figure 3.9).
2. The Web name option is already selected. Type **Painters**. Click on **OK** to confirm.

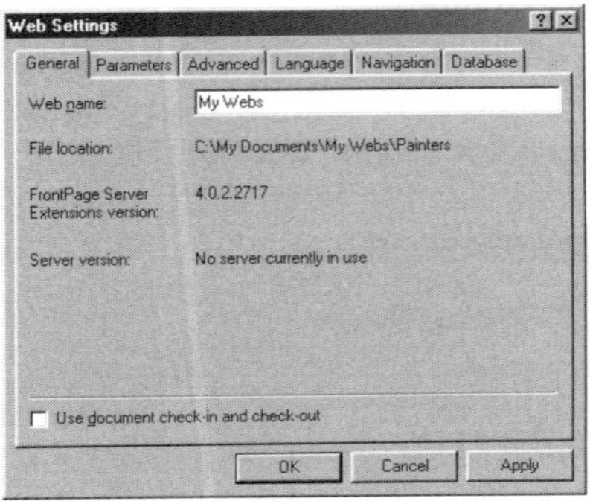

FrontPage 2000

Figure 3.9 Naming a site.

The new name is displayed in the Title bar (see Figure 3.10).

Figure 3.10: The name of the active site is displayed in the Title bar.

Closing a site

To close a site, click on **File, Close**. You can also press the **Ctrl+F4** keyboard keys.

The File, Close command is only available in the Page view.

Opening an existing site

Let us see now how to open a site which was already created.

*You can choose to automatically display the last Web in which you have worked since you last started FrontPage. To do this, click on **Tools, Options**, tick the **Open last Web automatically when FrontPage starts** option, then click on **OK** to confirm.*

3: Sites: creating and organising

To open an existing site:

1. Click on **File, Open Web** (see Figure 3.11).

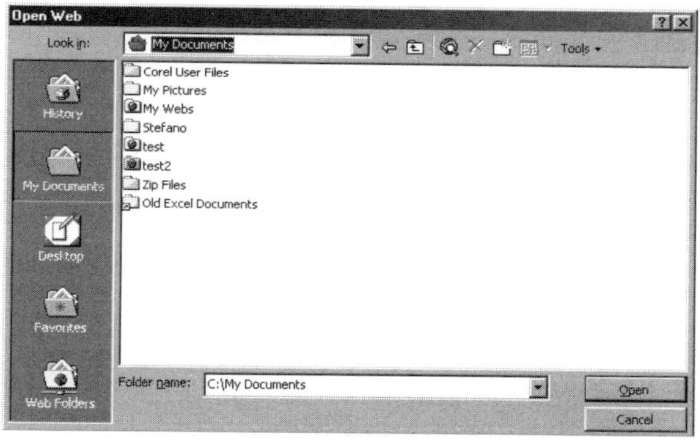

Figure 3.11 The Open dialog box lets you open a site quickly.

2. Click on the **Web Folders** icon to retrieve the tree structure. Double-click on the site that you wish to open. Click on the **Open** button.

> *To open the last site in which you have worked, click on **File**, **Recent Webs**. In the menu, click on the site you want to open.*

Deleting a site

If you no longer need a site, you can quickly remove it:

1. Click on the **Folders** view.
2. Right click on the directory or subdirectory in the Folder List, and then select **Delete** on the shortcut menu (see Figure 3.12).

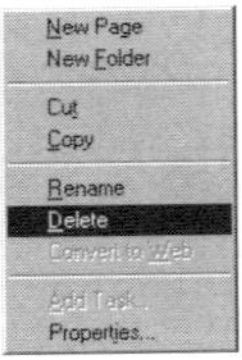

FrontPage 2000

Figure 3.12 The site context menu allows you to delete the site, but also to access its properties, to create a new folder or even to insert a new page.

3. A Confirm Delete dialog box is displayed (see Figure 3.13). You must specify what you want to delete.

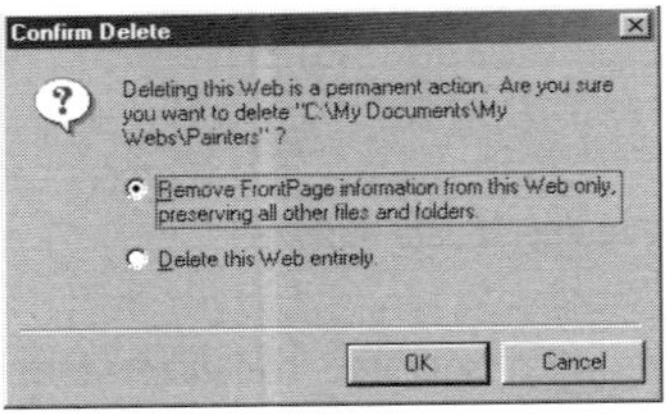

Figure 3.13 Specify the type of deletion you wish to carry out.

Remember that:

- The **Remove FrontPage information from this Web only, preserving all other files and folders** option allows you to keep the elements of the site even when it is deleted.
- The **Delete this Web entirely** option deletes the whole site (contents, structure, and so on).

4. Tick the required option, then click on **OK** to confirm.

3: Sites: creating and organising

■ Site settings

FrontPage offers several types of settings that you can easily customise.

Language

Office 2000 allows you to specify the language to be used in your work.

To choose the language for the server messages:

1. In the site, click on **Tools**, **Web Settings**.
2. Click on **Language** (see Figure 3.14). Select the language you wish to activate in the Server message language. Click on **OK** to confirm.

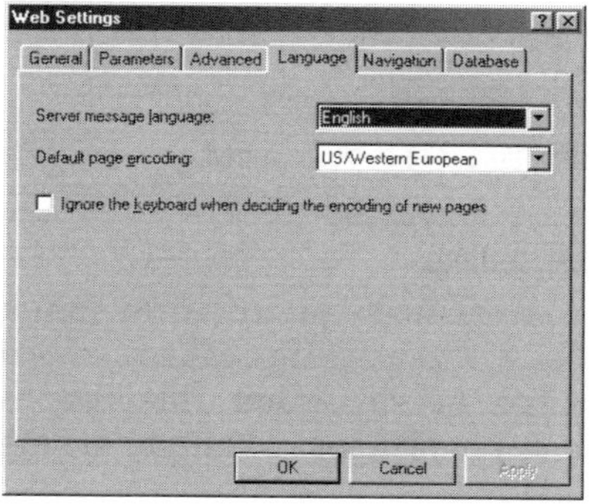

Figure 3.14 Choosing the language to be used in FrontPage.

Choice of the script language

If you already are an expert user, naturally you know scripting. FrontPage allows you to choose the scripting language to be activated.

FrontPage 2000

To choose the scripting language:

1. In the site, click on **Tools, Web Settings**.
2. Click on the **Advanced** tab (see Figure 3.15). Select the scripting language to activate in the Client option, then click on **OK** to confirm.

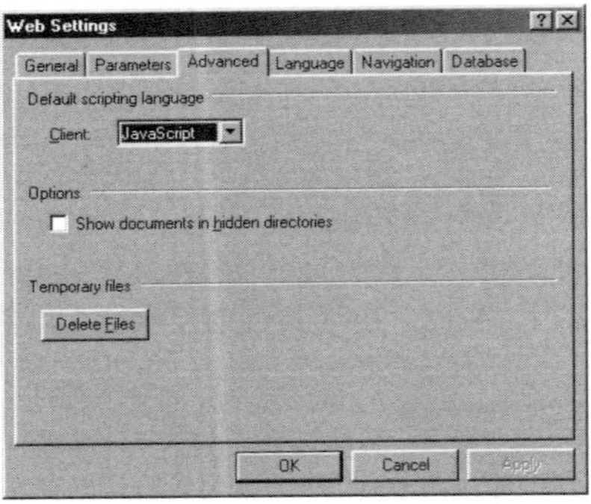

Figure 3.15 Choosing the scripting language to be activated.

Customising the navigation bar settings

The navigation bar is the strip usually placed at the top of the Web page, which allows you to navigate quickly between the various pages of the site. As the default, the previous pages are displayed under a specified name. You can modify these names.

To change the names in the navigation bar:

1. In the site, click on **Tools, Web Settings**.
2. Click on the **Navigation** tab. Customise the text labels as you wish. Click on **OK** to confirm.

3: Sites: creating and organising

■ Folder management

In the default setting, a normal site contains a page (index) and two folders (Private and Images). In Chapter 4, you will learn how to add pages to a site. For the purpose of our exercise, let us concentrate on folders.

To view the folders of the site that you have just created, click on **Folders** in the **Views** bar (see Figure 3.16).

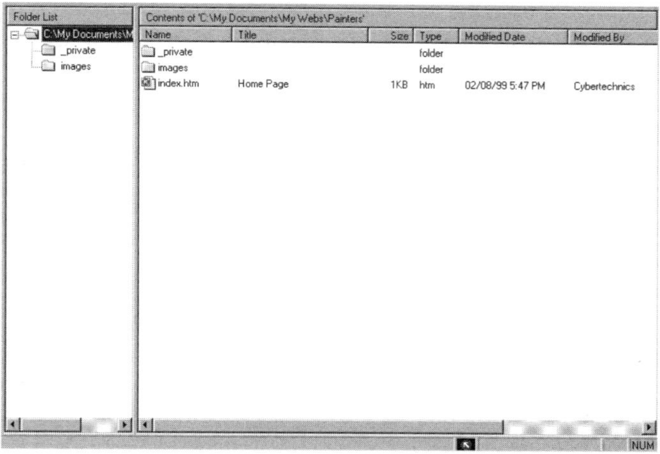

Figure 3.16 Viewing the folders contained in the site.

What is the Private folder for?

When you create a normal site or any other type of site, FrontPage automatically creates a folder called Private. This corresponds to a hidden folder, meaning that it will not be viewed by those who visit your site when it will be published on the Web. This folder allows you to store the returns of the forms that you may have created in your site (see Chapter 7).

FrontPage 2000

Folder creation

You can add folders to a site for a more precise organisation.

To create a new folder:

1. Right click on the directory or subdirectory in the Folder List. In our example, on C:\My documents\My Web sites\painters. Select **New folder**.

   A new folder is displayed in the area to the right.

2. Enter the name of the folder. In our example, type **Documents**. Repeat these procedures to create a second folder that you will call **Portraits**.

Deletion of folders

If you have created too many folders, you can quickly delete them. Just be careful not to delete files contained in a folder which you may need for other work.

To delete a folder:

1. Open the relevant site. Click on **Folders** in the **Views** bar.
2. Right click on the folder to be deleted, then select **Delete**. Confirm deletion by clicking on **OK** in the **Confirm Deletion** dialog box.

Renaming a folder

If you chose for your folders no longer matches their contents, you can rename them.

To rename a folder:

1. Open the relevant site. Click on **Folders** in the **Views** bar.
2. Right click on the folder, then select **Rename**. The name of the folder is displayed in highlight. Simply type the new name and press the **Enter** key to confirm.

4 Pages: how to create and organise them

- The page concept
- Folders view
- Page creation and management
- Page organisation
- Page settings
- Automatic page creation

In this chapter, we are going to see how to insert pages, delete them, name them, and so on. We will then learn how to define settings for the pages you have created.

■ The page concept

As we have already seen, a site contains one or more pages. You should be aware that the page concept is not at all the same as standard word-processing. In practice, on the Web, a page does not have a prescribed size, it can be a few lines or hundreds of lines long.

We are going to see in the following chapters how to insert text, pictures, format, and so on. For now, we are simply going to learn about the procedures for creating pages within the site.

Start Page

When you create a site, the start page is always the first page in the site. Because it is the first thing your visitors will see, it needs to be able to provide the basic information needed for them to find their way through your site.

Here are some of the golden rules for creating a start page:

- **Introduction function**. Since this is the first page your visitors will see, it must provide a brief summary of the site and of its author.
- **Information function**. The start page should provide your visitors with information on what they are likely to find in the following pages.
- **Navigation function**. Visitors should be able to go to all the other pages in the site with the links in the Start Page. Equally, each page in the site must allow to return quickly to the start page.

4: Pages: how to create and organise them

In our example, and in general, the index.htm page will be the start page for the site.

■ Folders view

In the course of this chapter, we will work mainly in the Folders view. We have already established that this view allows you to create, delete, copy or move folders or files (pages). Here are a number of hints for working better and more quickly in this view:

- To open the **Folders** view, click on its icon in the **Views** bar.
- To open a folder, double-click on the **Folders** icon (the small yellow rectangle) in the **Folder List**. The contents of the folder are displayed in the area to the right.
- To close a folder, double-click on the **Open folders** icon (the small yellow open rectangle) in the **Folder List**.

■ Page creation and management

Anything to do with creating, naming or deleting pages, is done in the Navigation view. This view displays the created pages in the shape of small rectangles and also allows you to see the structure of the site at a glance.

To display the **Navigation** view, click on it in the **Views** bar (see Figure 4.1).

At the moment, your site only contains a single page.

Insertion of fresh pages
Before inserting pages in your site, make sure that the Folder List is displayed. This allows you to insert pages quickly with the help of their context menu.

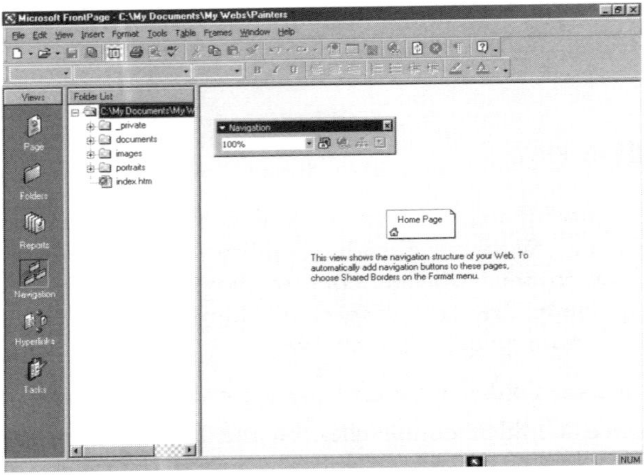

FrontPage 2000

Figure 4.1 Display the site in Navigation mode in order to view its structure.

To display the Folder List, click on the **Folder List** icon in the Standard toolbar (see Figure 4.2).

Figure 4.2 The Folder List displays the contents of the site.

4: Pages: how to create and organise them

We are now going to insert pages in our site, then place them in a folder.

To insert a page:

1. In the **Folder List,** right click on the directory or subdirectory. In our example, right click on **C:\My Documents\My Web site\ painters**.
2. Select **new page** from the menu. A new page is highlighted (see Figure 4.3) in the **Folder List**. Press the **Enter** key to confirm.

The page format for the site is .htm.

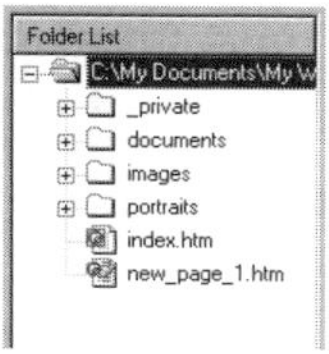

Figure 4.3 The new page is inserted underneath the existing page.

In our example, insert three additional pages to obtain the structure as shown in Figure 4.4.

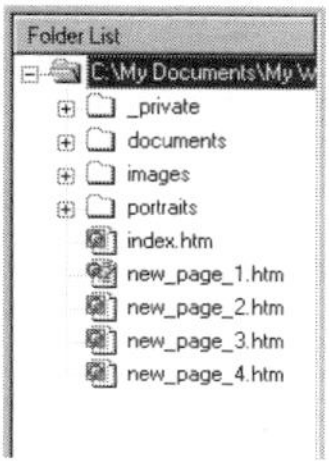

Figure 4.4 Your site should contain a total of five pages.

FrontPage 2000

> *You can also insert template pages or style sheets. To find out how to do this, refer to the section on Style sheets and Template pages (pp. 65 - 66).*

Opening a page

When you have inserted new pages into your site, you must be able to work with them: inserting text (see Chapter 5), inserting pictures (see Chapter 7), formatting (see Chapter 6), and so on. To do this, you must display the page in the Page view. For this you have two options:

- In the **Folders** view, double-click on the relevant page in the area to the right.
- In any view, click on **File, Open** (see Figure 4.5). In the dialog box, click on the page you wish to open, then on **Open**. The page is displayed in the Page view.

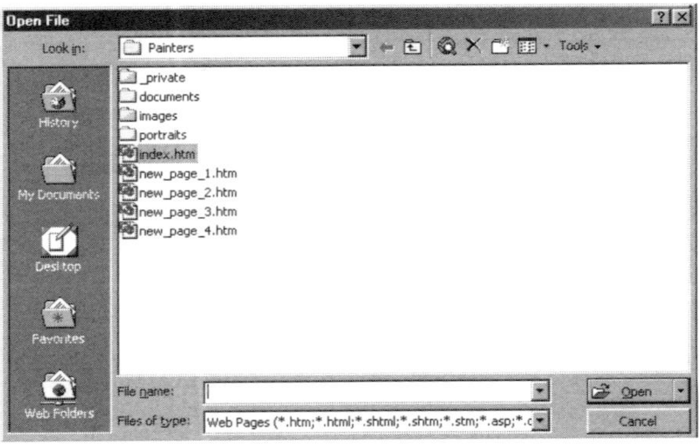

Figure 4.5 In the Open File dialog box, you can choose the page you want to open.

4: Pages: how to create and organise them

Naming a page

You have seen that, when you insert a fresh page, this is automatically named by FrontPage as new_page_N°.htm. We must accept that this is not going be sufficiently clear.

To rename a page:

1. Display the **Folders** view. Right click on the page to be renamed. In our example, right click on **new_page_1.htm** and select **rename**.

   The name of the page is highlighted.

2. Enter the new name. In our example, type history.htm. It is very important not to forget the extension.

   A dialog box is displayed, confirming that the page has been renamed.

3. Repeat the procedures to rename **new_page_2.htm** to table.htm, **new_page_3.htm** to opinion.htm and **new_page_4.htm** to monet.htm. You must get the same configuration as shown in Figure 4.6.

Name	Title	Size	Type	Modified Date	Modified By
_private			folder		
documents			folder		
images			folder		
portraits			folder		
index.htm	Home Page	1KB	htm	03/08/99 9:41 AM	Cybertechnics
history.htm	history.htm	1KB	htm	03/08/99 11:01 AM	Cybertechnics
table.htm	table.htm	1KB	htm	03/08/99 11:00 AM	Cybertechnics
opinion.htm	opinion.htm	1KB	htm	03/08/99 11:01 AM	Cybertechnics
monet.htm	monet.htm	1KB	htm	03/08/99 11:02 AM	Cybertechnics

Contents of 'C:\My Documents\My Webs\Painters'

Figure 4.6 Renamed site pages.

Deleting a page

When you think that some pages are no longer needed, just delete them. Be aware that only the text and the page will be deleted: the pictures present in the page will remain in the folder.

To delete a page in the **Folders** view, right click on the relevant page and select **Delete**. In the dialog box which is displayed (see Figure 4.7), click on the **Yes** button to confirm.

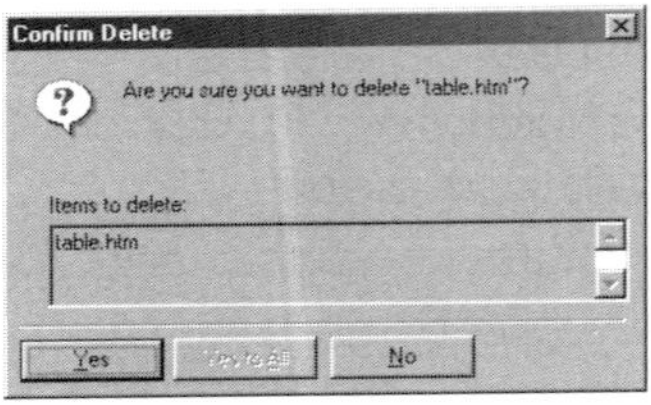

Figure 4.7 Confirm deletion of the page.

Saving a page

As opposed to the site itself which you do not need to save, pages must be saved. As soon as you have carried out a modification, or you have inserted a new element and so on, remember to save it.

To save a page, click on **File**, **Save**. You can also click on the **Save** icon (with the symbol of a diskette) in the Standard toolbar.

Closing a page

When you have worked in a page and you have saved it, you can close it by clicking on **File**, **Close** in the Page view.

If you have not saved your page before closing it, FrontPage opens a dialog box which prompts you to save the changes.

4: Pages: how to create and organise them

Print Preview

Before printing a page, you should view it in order to assess the way it looks. The Print Preview function displays the whole page and allows you to modify the display to give you a better view of the effects you have created.

In the relevant page, click on **File, Print Preview** (see Figure 4.8). Click on the **Close** button when you have finished.

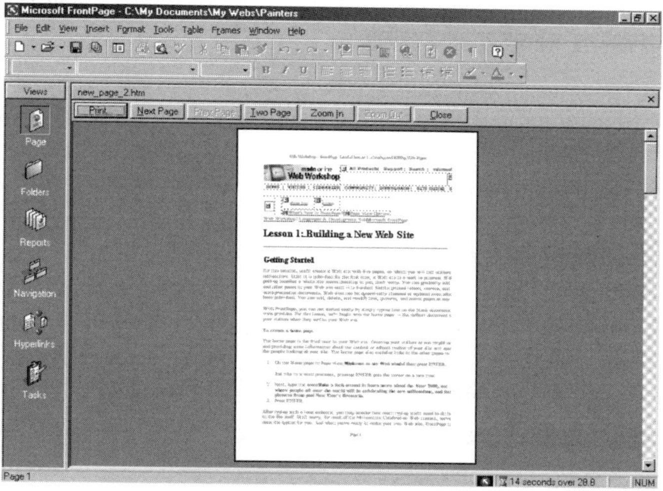

Figure 4.8 Print Preview of a page of the site.

Formatting before printing

If you want to insert a header, a footer, or page numbers, you must indicate your choices in the Page Setup command.

To carry out formatting:

1. In the relevant page, click on **File, Page Setup** (see Figure 4.9).

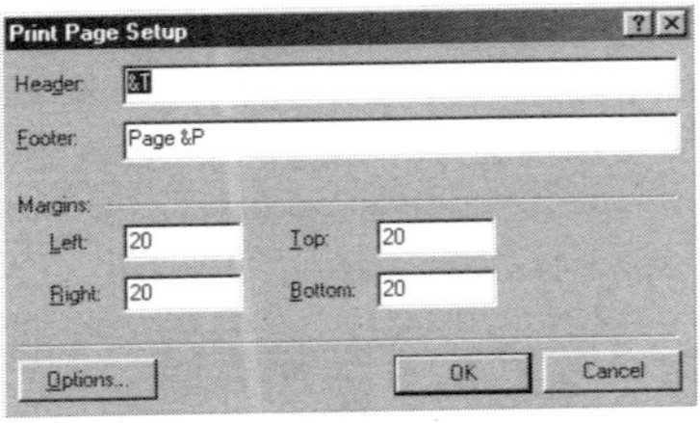

FrontPage 2000

Figure 4.9 The Print Page Setup dialog box allows you to choose various formatting options before printing.

2. If you wish, you can type the header in the relevant box or the footer, again in the relevant box. Define the various margins.
3. Click on **OK** to confirm.

Printing a page

To print a page:

1. In the relevant page and in the **Page** view, click on the **Print** icon (with the symbol of a small printer) in the Standard toolbar. You can also click on **File, Print** (see Figure 4.10).

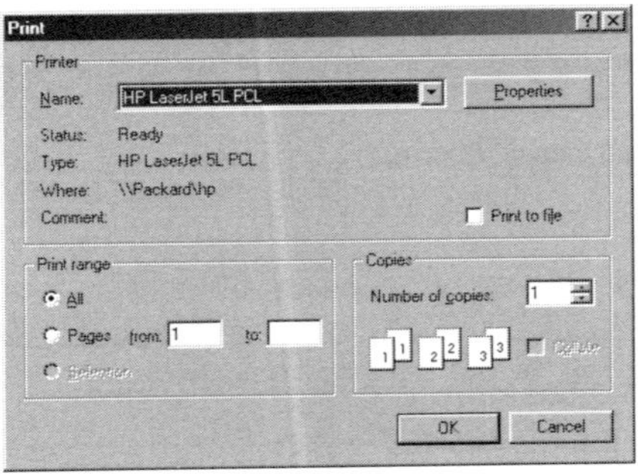

Figure 4.10 The Print dialog box allows you to define the print options, then to start printing.

4: Pages: how to create and organise them

2. In the **Print** dialog box, define the print range, the number of copies, the printer to be used and so on, then click on **OK**.

Viewing in the browser

If it is true that print preview is very useful, it must be said that a Web page is really meant to be published on the Internet and not printed. It would therefore be better to assess the success of the page in the browser. You will get an accurate idea as to the impression it will make when published.

To view a page in the browser:

1. In the relevant page and in **Page** view, click on the **Preview** tab. If you want to see the page exactly as it will look in a browser (Internet Explorer or Netscape Communicator), click on **File, Preview in Browser**.

   The default browser in your computer is displayed (see Figure 4.11).

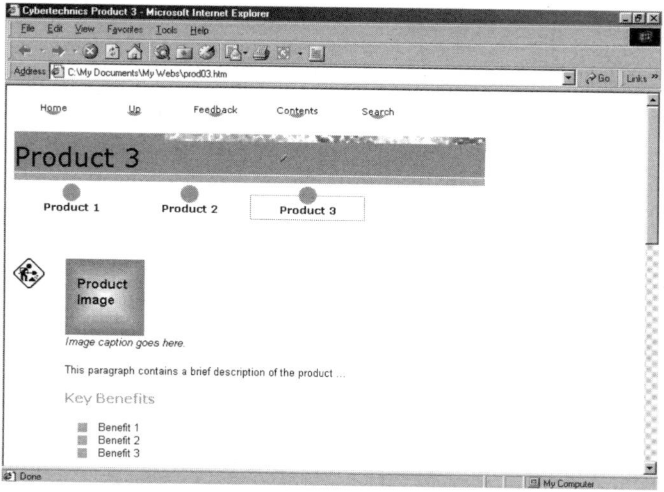

Figure 4.11 The browser allows you to view the site exactly as it will look on the Web.

FrontPage 2000

2. When you have viewed the page, click on **File, Close Web**, then return to FrontPage.

■ Page organisation

It is important to organise the site and the pages properly so that it will be easier to work with them. This is a crucial stage before creating pages. In the following chapters you will be shown how to define the order of appearance of pages and how to link them with hyperlinks.

Placing pages in a folder

When you have created several pages for your site, you need to place them in their assigned folders. This way, the site will be perfectly organised and you can start creating the contents of the pages.

To place pages in a folder:

1. Click on **Folders** in the **Views** bar.

   At the moment, the pages are in the **Painters** web folder. Put them in the **Documents** folder.

2. Click on the **History.htm** page in the area to the right. Keeping the button pressed, drag it into the **Documents** folder (see Figure 4.12). Release the button. The page is now in the **Documents** folder. Repeat the same procedures for all the other pages of the site.

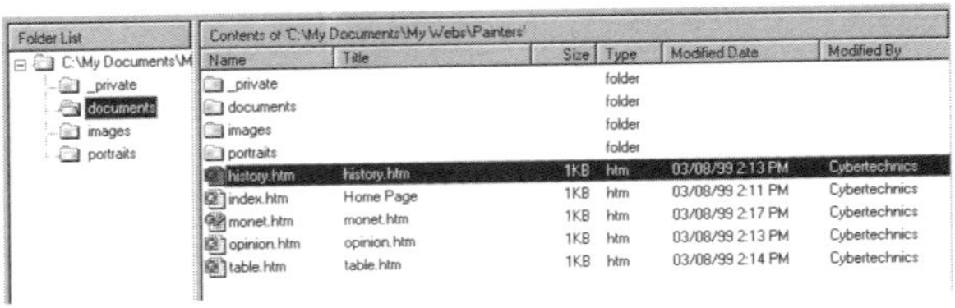

Figure 4.12 Moving the pages to the Documents folder.

4: Pages: how to create and organise them

■ Page settings

Just as for the site, you can define a number of settings for each page. We have already seen some of these settings, such as the definition of the HTML source and the colour of codes in Chapter 2. Other settings will be introduced in the following chapters.

Defining spell checking

We are going to see in the next chapter that FrontPage underlines spelling errors with a thin wavy red line, as in Word, PowerPoint and so on. As the default, this option is active. But, if you wish, you can deactivate this option and choose not to be shown errors while you are creating the page:

1. In the relevant page, in **Page** view, click on **Tools, Page Options**. Click on the **General** tab (see Figure 4.13).

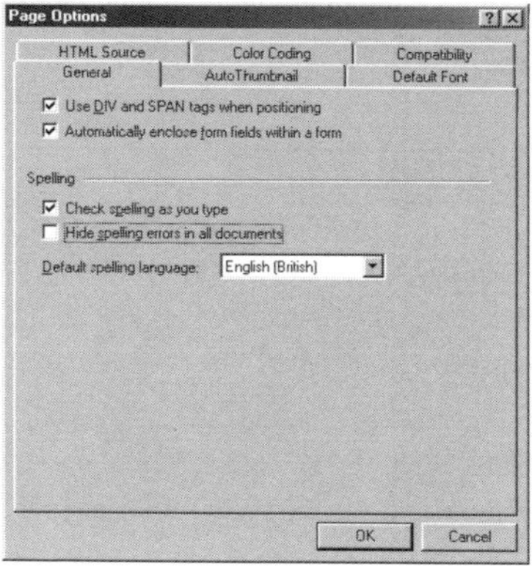

Figure 4.13 You can choose not to show spelling errors while you are creating the page.

2. Click on the **Hide spelling errors in all documents** check box to activate it. Click on **OK** to confirm.

FrontPage 2000

Defining the target browser

You will certainly be aware that, competition being what it is, a fair number of sites are displayed differently according to the type of browser used by the visitor. It is a pity, but this is the way things are at the moment. FrontPage 2000 is aware that this creates problems for authors of sites, who go to a lot of trouble to create effects which are only going to be visible with one of the browsers on the market. Therefore, FrontPage 2000 allows you to target the browser. This way, you will be able to choose functions which are fully compatible with the browser you select. This is obviously extremely useful, so you will not be wasting time including functions which do not work with the target browser.

To target your browser:

1. In the relevant page, in **Page** view, click on **Tools, Page Options**. Click on the **Compatibility** tab (see Figure 4.14).

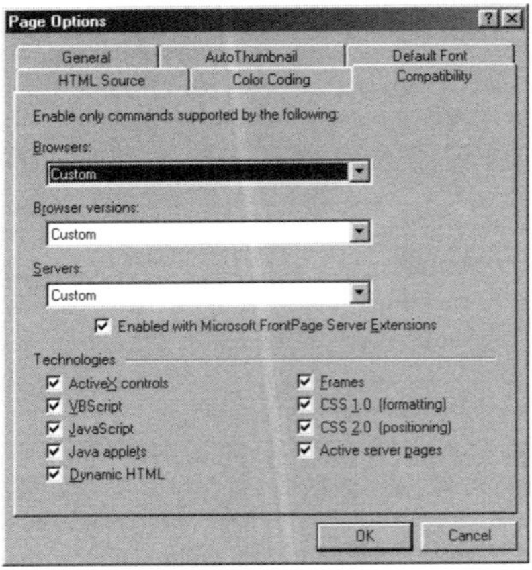

Figure 4.14 Specify the target Browser type and version.

2. Click on the little arrow in the **Browser** box, then select the browser you want. Click on the little arrow in the

4: Pages: how to create and organise them

Browser versions, then select the version you want. Activate and/or deactivate the various options in **Technologies**. Click on **OK** to confirm.

■ Automatic page creation

At the beginning of this chapter you learnt how to create a new page. You are now going to see that FrontPage allows you to create pages from a template or from a style sheet.

Creating pages with a template

You are certainly aware of what a template is and what it is for: it allows you to create a page, a table and so on, quickly, from an existing template, by simply modifying the text format. FrontPage offers this type of tool to speed up the creation of a Web page. When you have created a new page with a template, fill the various text boxes, then save: the page is created!

To choose a page with a template:

1. Click on **File, New, Page**. Then click on the **General** tab (see Figure 4.15).

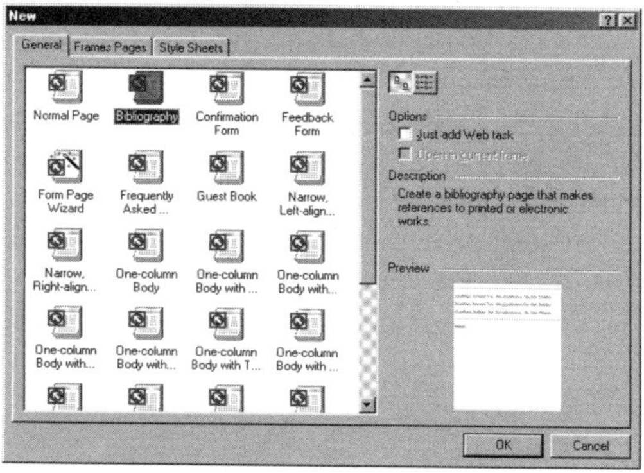

Figure 4.15 Creating a page quickly with a FrontPage template.

2. The first choice, **Normal Page**, creates a blank page. All the other choices are templates. If you want to know what a template does, simply click it and read the description in the area to the right. To select a template, double-click on it.

Style Sheets

A style contains formatting information (see Chapter 5 and 6) such as font, colour background, border, and so on. A style sheet therefore includes a set of style definitions which can be applied to elements on one or on several pages. There are various types of formatting options: font effects, page breaks, paragraph properties, order, frame and position.

In its version 2000, FrontPage provides a number of cascading style sheets which let you format your site very quickly.

The cascading style sheet technology, also called CSS (Cascading Style Sheet), is usually compatible with the most currently used browsers, such as Internet Explorer, from version 3.0, and Netscape Navigator, from version 4.0.

To apply a style sheet to a page, a text, and so on:

1. Display the page or select the relevant text (see the formatting section), click on **File, New, Page**. Click on the **Style Sheets** tab (see Figure 4.16).
2. The first option, **Normal Style Sheet**, creates a blank cascading style sheet which you can define later. All the other options are styles. To know exactly what type of style each one applies, simply click on it, then read the description in the area to the right. To select a style sheet, double-click on it.

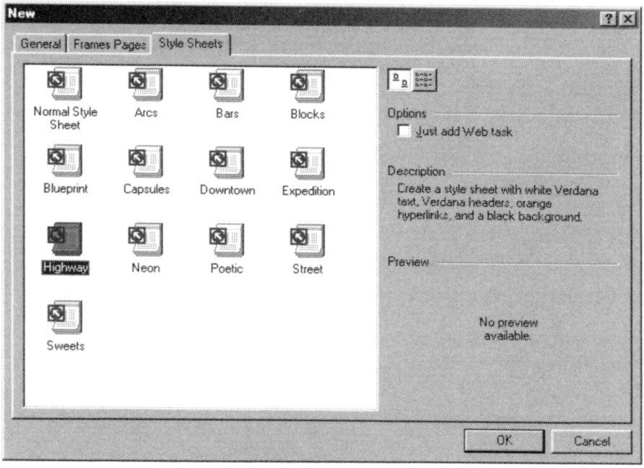

4: Pages: how to create and organise them

Figure 4.16 Quick page formatting with a style sheet.

5 Text

Page view
Entering text
Moving within the text
Inserting files
Selecting text
Editing text
Undo/Redo an action
Other pages in your site

Now that you have created your site and your pages, you need to enter your text, place your pictures, and apply the formatting. We will now see how to enter text, insert text files, move within the text, modify it, and so on.

■ Page view

In this chapter, you will mainly work in Page view. In the first chapter you have seen that this view allows you to create, conceive and modify Web pages. As you type your text, add images, insert tables, form fields and other elements to your page, Page view displays these elements as they will appear in the browser.

To work in Page view:

- To open **Page** view, click on its icon in the **Views** bar.
- To open a page, click on the **Open** icon (the small open yellow rectangle) in the Standard toolbar. In the dialog box which is displayed, double click on the page to open it.
- To close a page, click on the **Close** icon (with the symbol of an X) in the **Title** bar of the folder.
- To navigate between two open pages, click on **Window** and select the page you want to display as first level.

■ Entering text

These are some of the rules and tips you will need to know when entering text:

- As the default, the blinking cursor, or insertion point, indicates the point where the text you are going to enter will be positioned.

5: Text

- Just carry on typing: FrontPage goes automatically to the next line when you reach the right margin.
- To create a new paragraph, press the **Enter** key. This procedure also allows you to insert a blank line.
- To go to a new line without creating a new paragraph, press the **Shift+Enter** keyboard keys.
- Avoid using the tab keyboard key to create indents in the text. It is better to manage this feature with returns or, better still, with columns (see Chapter 9).

Non-printable characters

When you create paragraphs, or insert blank lines, FrontPage generates characters called non-printable characters. To view them, click on the button with the **Show All** symbol in the Standard toolbar (see Figure 5.1).

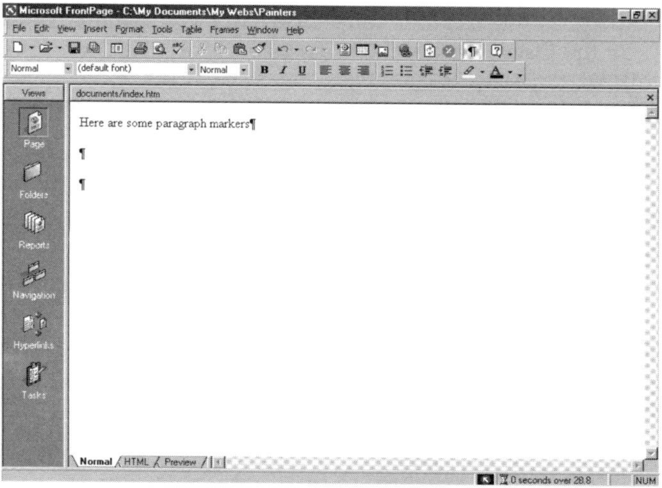

Figure 5.1 The button represented by a Pi allows you to display paragraph markers.

FrontPage 2000

Non-breaking hyphenation and accented uppercase characters

When you are typing, FrontPage goes automatically to the new line. If there are words which should not be split, and to avoid the program inserting the first word on one line and the second on another, you must create a non-breaking space or non-breaking hyphenation.

To create a forced space, type the first word, press the **Ctrl+Shift+Space bar** keyboard keys. Enter the second word and again press **Ctrl+Shift+Space bar**.

When you type titles or any other text in uppercase, FrontPage does not display accents. For a more sophisticated presentation, you can create titles with accented uppercase.

To insert accented uppercase characters:

1. Click on **Insert, Symbol** (see Figure 5.2).
2. Click on the accented uppercase letter you require. Click on the **Insert** button, then **Close**.

Figure 5.2 Use symbols to insert accented uppercase characters.

Text in the start page

You are going to start creating your start page for your site. This page is called Index.

To create your start page:

1. Click on **Folders** view, then the **Documents** folder.
2. Double-click on **Index.htm**.

    The page is displayed in **Page** view.

5: Text

3. You must enter the following text next, keeping the page breaks as they are indicated:

   Impressions of impressionism.

   You will certainly have heard of impressionist painters, but do you actually know their history? Discover it on this site.

   Summary.

   History.

   Their best works of art.

   The father of impressionism or Monet and all his periods.

   Your taste in matter of paintings.

   A walk through museums.

4. You must achieve what is shown in Figure 5.3. Remember to save the page by clicking on the **Save** icon in the Standard toolbar.

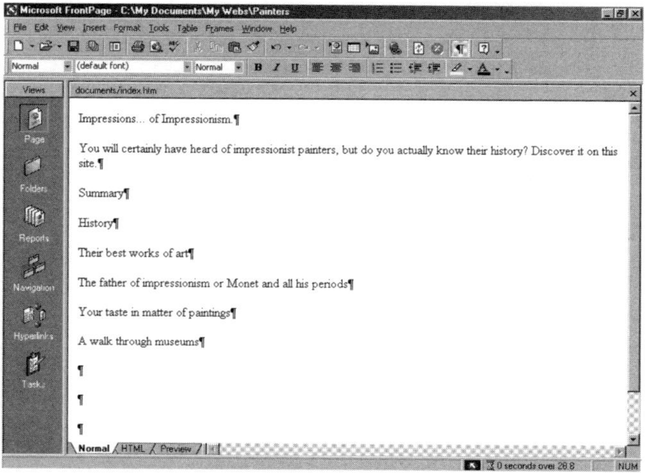

Figure 5.3 Text in your start page.

FrontPage 2000

Inserting a blank line

A blank line allows you to give some space to the text. You can of course achieve the same result by changing spacing between paragraphs (see Chapter 6).

To insert a blank line in the text of the start page, click on the line end 'Discover it on this site', then press the **Enter** key.

■ Moving within the text

There are various ways to move within a text:

- Point to where you wish to go, then click.
- Drag the horizontal or vertical scroll bar in the required direction (up, down, left or right). A balloon is displayed: it indicates the number of the page which will be displayed if you release the mouse (see Figure 5.4).

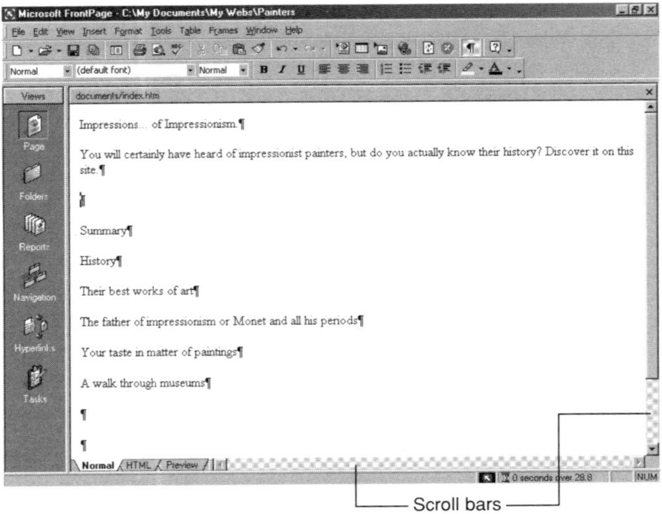

Figure 5.4 Use the scroll bars to display the required page.

5: Text

- Click on one of the arrows positioned at the bottom of the vertical scroll bar to scroll the text up or down. Release the mouse button when the required text is displayed.

Moving quickly within the text

As well as the mouse and four direction arrows, FrontPage offers a number of key combinations to move quickly within the text (see Table 5.1).

Action	Keys
Go to the end of the current line	End
Go to the top of the current line	Home
Go to the top of the document	Ctrl+Home
Go to the end of the document	Ctrl+End
Go to the top of the first line in the screen	Ctrl+Page Up
Go to the end of the first line in the screen	Ctrl+Page Down
Go to the top of the previous paragraph	Ctrl+Arrow up
Go to the top of the next paragraph	Ctrl+Arrow down
Go to the beginning of the previous word	Ctrl+Arrow left
Go to the beginning of the next word	Ctrl+Arrow right

Table 5.1 Moving quickly within the text.

FrontPage 2000

■ Inserting files

FrontPage allows you to insert text saved under another format into your page. You can import various types of files, such as text only, HTML files, .doc (Word files), .xls (Excel files), and so on.

When you import a word-processing file (.doc, text only, and so on), the Page view maintains all the formats recognised by the Web pages (bold, italic, underlined, and so on), but complex formats are likely to be ignored.

Creating a text file

You are going to create a text file in Word which you will then insert in the History page of your site.

To create a text file:

1. Click on **Start, Programs, Microsoft Word** in the Windows Desktop.
2. In the file, type the following text:

   A LITTLE BIT OF HISTORY

   In the beginning...

   We could see that a new impressionist school was on the cards in 1860, when a revolution in landscape painting, occured: landscapes stopped being simply a background and became instead the subject of the painting.

   In 1863, Monet, Renoir, Sisley and Bazille left their studio in Paris and moved to Chailly-in-Bière. All their paintings conform to the same ideals of simplicity, colour and light.

   The impressionist exhibition

   It was in 1874 that the term impressionism was finally coined up to then, the movement by painters such as Monet, Sisley, Degas, Berthe, Morisot and Cézanne, was

5: Text

called the 'Open Air School', and then 'The Independants'. The name came from Monet's painting, Impressions of the Rising Sun, now at the Marmottant Museum in Paris.

Having failed to convince the jury of the Exhibition which was held every year, they ended up showing their work in fringe exhibitions; and this is how the first official Impressionist exhibition started, in 1874. The exhibition was presented in the years 1876, 1877, 1879, 1882.

Harshly ridiculed at the beginning, little by little they managed to win the critical acclaim and the support of some famous writers, such as Emile Zola. The impressionist movement ended in 1882, and was followed by the Neo-impressionism and the Fauvist school, represented by painters such as Vincent Van Gogh.

Impressionist painting

Impressionism is about painting the countryside, water, and so on. Each painter dedicated himself to the study of a specific theme, for instance, the sky, the variations of the light, of seasons, of the hours in the day. Under different lighting, shadows take on colours, the sun becomes iridescent and white becomes bluish, creating a true natural impression. This movement only lasted for eight short years, but produced scores of masterpieces. Monet, one of the most prolific painters within the movement, said of his paintings: 'No, I am not a great painter or a great poet. I only know that I'm doing my best to express what I feel when faced with nature.'

The main impressionist painters

Monet

Degas

Manet

FrontPage 2000

```
Sisley

Morisot

Renoir

Cézanne
```

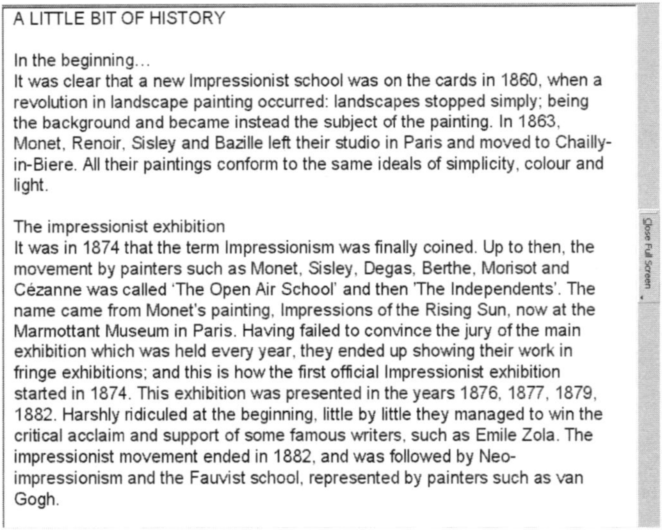

> A LITTLE BIT OF HISTORY
>
> In the beginning...
> It was clear that a new Impressionist school was on the cards in 1860, when a revolution in landscape painting occurred: landscapes stopped simply; being the background and became instead the subject of the painting. In 1863, Monet, Renoir, Sisley and Bazille left their studio in Paris and moved to Chailly-in-Biere. All their paintings conform to the same ideals of simplicity, colour and light.
>
> The impressionist exhibition
> It was in 1874 that the term Impressionism was finally coined. Up to then, the movement by painters such as Monet, Sisley, Degas, Berthe, Morisot and Cézanne was called 'The Open Air School' and then 'The Independents'. The name came from Monet's painting, Impressions of the Rising Sun, now at the Marmottant Museum in Paris. Having failed to convince the jury of the main exhibition which was held every year, they ended up showing their work in fringe exhibitions; and this is how the first official Impressionist exhibition started in 1874. This exhibition was presented in the years 1876, 1877, 1879, 1882. Harshly ridiculed at the beginning, little by little they managed to win the critical acclaim and support of some famous writers, such as Emile Zola. The impressionist movement ended in 1882, and was followed by Neo-impressionism and the Fauvist school, represented by painters such as van Gogh.

Figure 5.5 This is part of the text file that you created.

3. You must achieve what is shown in Figure 5.5. Click on **File, Save As.** Name the file **History**. Click on **File, Quit** to close Word.

To insert a file in the Web page:

1. Click on the **Open** icon in the Standard toolbar.
2. Double-click on **History**. Click on **Insert, File** (see Figure 5.6).

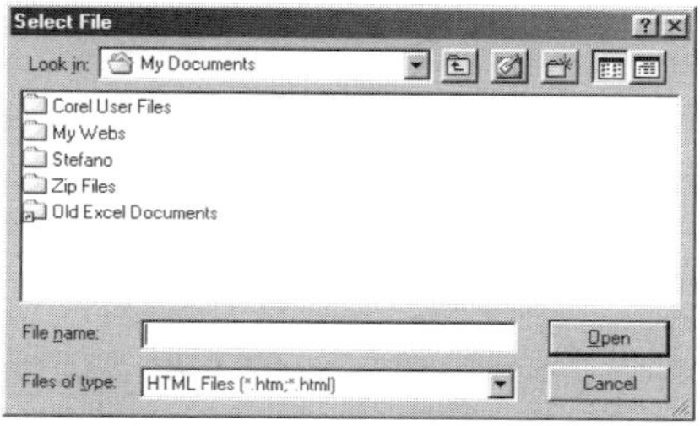

5: Text

Figure 5.6 The Select File dialog box allows you to find the file to be inserted.

3. Click on the arrow of the **Look in** option and select the folder containing the file called **History**. Click on the arrow of the **File of type** option and select **Word 97 – 2000**. Double-click on the file **History**. Click on **File, Save**. The text file is displayed in the page (see Figure 5.7).

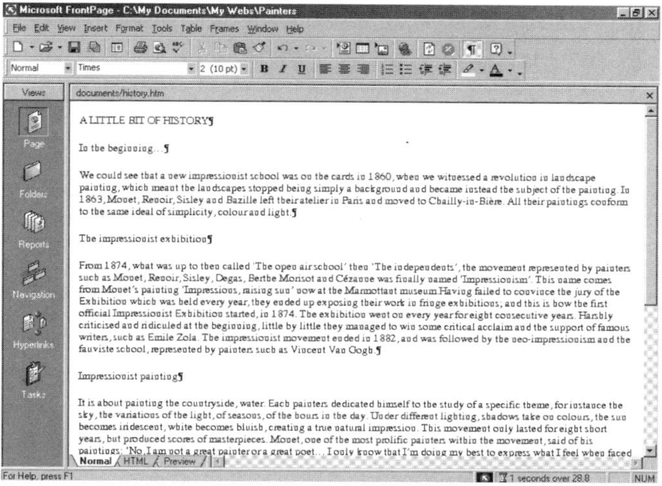

Figure 5.7 The text file that you have created in Word is displayed in the History page.

■ Selecting text

Before processing text (moving it, copying, deleting, and so on), or to implement formatting, you must first select it. This means selecting the text to which you want to apply a format. A selected text is highlighted (reversed out).

> *To select a word, click on the top of the word, then drag the mouse on it, keeping the mouse button pressed. Alternatively a word can be selected by double-clicking on it.*

To select a group of words, click in front of the first word to be selected, press the **Shift** key, then, keeping the key pressed, use the direction keyboard keys.

To clear a selection, click outside it.

Once selected, the text is highlighted. FrontPage, like other Microsoft applications, offers you a quick text selection function (see Table 5.2).

Selection	Action
A word	Double-click on the word.
A sentence	Hold down the Ctrl key, then click on the sentence.
A line	Click to the left of the line.
A paragraph	Triple-click in the paragraph or double-click to its left.
The document	Press Ctrl+A

Table 5.2 Quick selection.

5: Text

■ Editing text

Once you have entered your text, you can insert additional text, replace a word or delete a word.

- To insert a word or a character in a text, click where you wish to insert it, then type the new word.
- To replace a word, double-click on it, then type the new word.
- To delete the text, select it, then press the **Del** key.
- To clear the text in front of the insertion point, press the **Backspace** key.
- To clear the text which is after the insertion point, press on the **Del** key.

■ Undo/Redo an action

To undo an action or a command that you have just executed, click on **Edit**, **Undo** (followed by the command name). If you wish to undo several commands, click on **Edit**, **Undo** as many times as necessary. You can also click on the **Undo** icon (the left-pointing arrow).

The reverse operation is also possible. For example, if you have undone an action that you want to preserve, use the Redo command.

To redo an action that you have just undone, click on **Edit**, **Redo** (followed by the command name). You can also click on the **Undo** icon (the right-pointing arrow).

FrontPage 2000

■ Other pages in your site

You are now going to enter text for other pages.

To create the text for the Monet page:

1. In the **Folders** view, double-click on the **Monet** page.
2. Enter the following text (see Figure 5.8):

   Claude Monet (1840-1926), father of the impressionism

   His picture 'Impressions of the rising sun' (1874)
   which gives the Impressionist movement its name.

3. Click on **File, Save**.

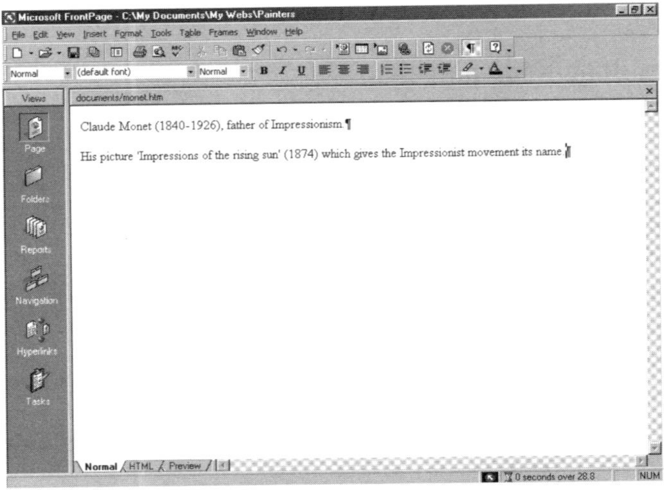

Figure 5.8 Keying in text for the Monet page.

5: Text

To create the text of the Paintings page (see Figure 5.9):

1. In the **Folders** view, double click on the **Painting** page.
2. Enter the next text:

   ```
   Main paintings
   
   Vincent Van Gogh, true heir
   ```

3. Click on **File, Save**.

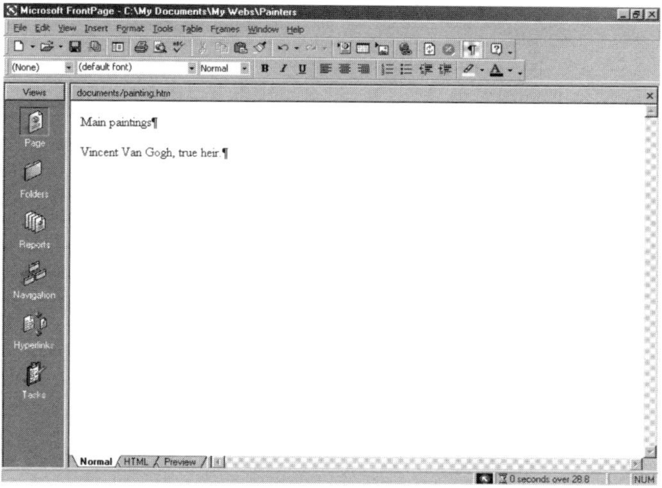

Figure 5.9 Keying text for the Paintings page.

6 Text: formatting

Formatting procedures
Formatting characters
Defining fonts by default
Changing case
Formatting paragraphs
Borders and shading
Format painting

In this chapter, we will learn all the formatting procedures available in FrontPage to enhance your text, enlarge it, reduce it, add colour to it, and so on. All the formats are executed in Page view.

■ Formatting procedures

You can define characters and paragraph formats before or after you start keying in your text:

- **Formatting before you start keying in your text**: select the various formats as shown in this chapter, then type the text.
- **Format after you start keying in your text**: select the text, then choose the formats you require.

■ Formatting characters

Formatting characters means assigning them a style (size, font, colour, and so on). The quality of a Web page is highly dependent on the way it looks, and this is why text formatting is so important.

■ Defining fonts by default

In FrontPage, the default proportional font is Times New Roman, the default fixed-width font is Courier New, both in 12-point size. To avoid having to modify the font on each page, you can choose to modify the default font. In this way, all text you enter in the site will be in the font of your choice.

6: Text: formatting

To modify the default font:

1. Click on **Tools, Page Options**. Click on **Default Font** (see Figure 6.1).

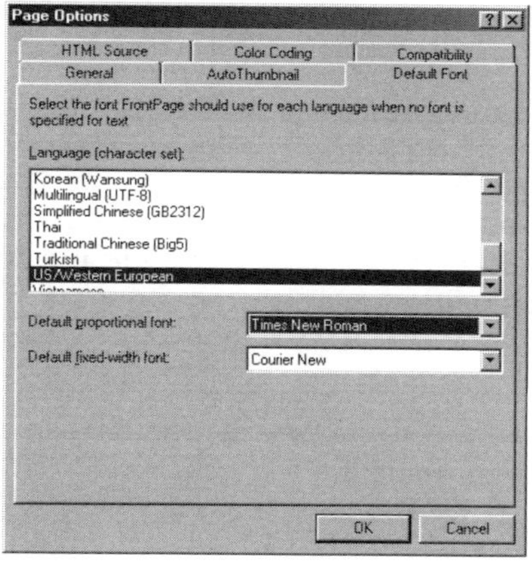

Figure 6.1 Choosing the font to activate by default in the site.

2. Click on the arrow of the **Default proportional font** option, then select the font to be activated. Repeat this procedure in the **Default fixed-width font** option. Click on **OK** to confirm.

Font modification

(default font) ▼ FrontPage allows you to modify the text font in a drop-down list in the Format toolbar.

To modify the font for a text:

1. Select the text to be modified. Click on the arrow in the **Font** drop-down list in the Standard toolbar (see Figure 6.2). In the **Index** start page for our site, select all the text.

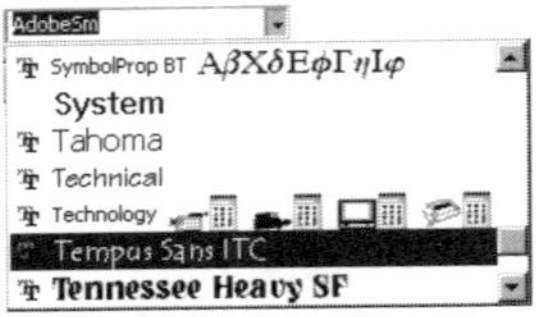

FrontPage 2000

[figure: font selection dropdown showing AdobeSm, SymbolProp BT AβXδEφΓηIφ, System, Tahoma, Technical, Technology, Tempus Sans ITC, Tennessee Heavy SF]

Figure 6.2 Select the font you'd like to use from the scrolling list.

2. Select the font to assign to the selected text. In our site, click on the **Tempus Sans ITC**. Click outside the selection. Repeat the same procedure for each page in the site and do not forget to save the modifications.

Modification of the font size

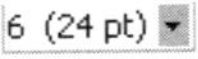

6 (24 pt) ▼ FrontPage allows you to modify the font size in a drop-down list in the Format toolbar.

To modify the size of a text:

1. Select the text to be modified. Click on the arrow of the **Font Size** drop-down list in the Standard toolbar (see Figure 6.3). Select the page title in the **Index** start page for our site.

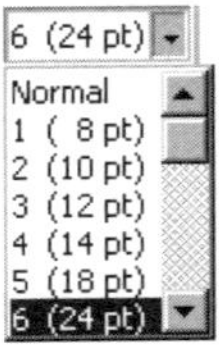

[figure: Font Size dropdown showing 6 (24 pt), Normal, 1 (8 pt), 2 (10 pt), 3 (12 pt), 4 (14 pt), 5 (18 pt), 6 (24 pt)]

Figure 6.3 In the Font Size drop-down list, select the size you wish to apply to the selected text.

2. Select the font size to apply to the selected text. In our site, click on size **6 (24pt)**. Click outside the selection. Then select all the text and apply size **5 (18pt)**. Repeat the same procedures for each page in the site (title in 24pt and text

6: Text: formatting

in 18pt). Also, in the **Index** and **History** pages, apply size **6 (24pt)** to the Summary title and to text with paragraphs (In the beginning, The impressionist exhibition, and so on). Save the modifications.

■ Changing case

The case of a character is a term which dates back to early printing times. Lower case corresponds to normal characters, upper case corresponds to capital letters. Changing the character case therefore consists in balancing uppercase with lower case, and vice versa.

To modify the page breaks characters:

1. Select the text to be modified. Click on **Format, Font** in the Standard toolbar (see Figure 6.4). In the **Index** start page for our site, select the page title.

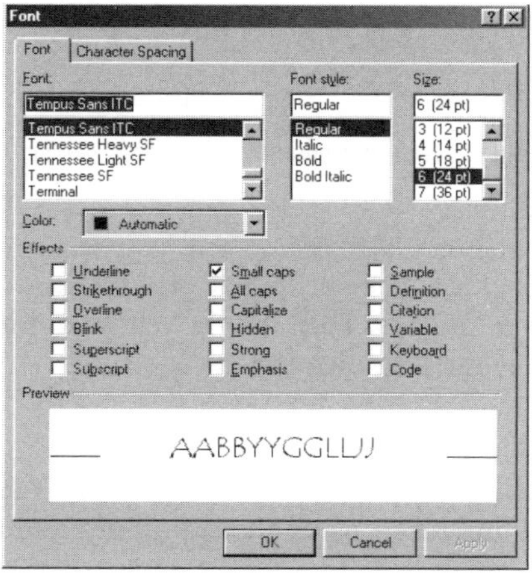

Figure 6.4 Defining the character case.

FrontPage 2000

2. In the Effects area, click on the check box which corresponds to your choice. In our site, click on the **Small caps** option, then on **OK** to confirm. Repeat the same procedures for each title in the site. Save the modifications.

Adding colour to the text

FrontPage allows you to display your text in colour. This procedure is extremely quick to execute. With a few clicks, you can add colour to your page and make it more attractive. To modify the colour of the text, you can use the Font colour icon, in the Format toolbar.

To modify the text colour:

1. Select the text to be coloured. Click on the arrow of the **Font Colour** icon in the Standard toolbar (see Figure 6.5). In the **Index** start page in our site, select the page title.

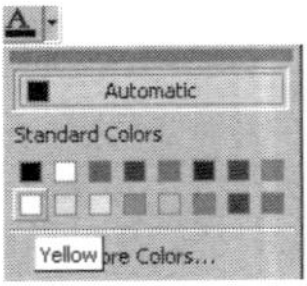

Figure 6.5 Selecting a colour in the context menu in the icon Font colour.

2. In the tool context menu, select the colour you wish to apply. For our site, click on **Yellow**. Repeat the same procedures for each title in the site. Then, apply **Yellow** to the text for all pages. Save the modifications.

Defining a customised colour

In its 2000 version, FrontPage can customise colours. You are therefore no longer limited to using the standard colour palette and can in fact create a colour which matches perfectly what you want.

6: Text: formatting

To define a customised colour:

1. Select the text to be coloured. Click on the Font colour icon arrow in the Standard toolbar.

2. In the tool context menu, click on **More colors** (see Figure 6.6). In the prism, click on the colour block which corresponds to your choice.

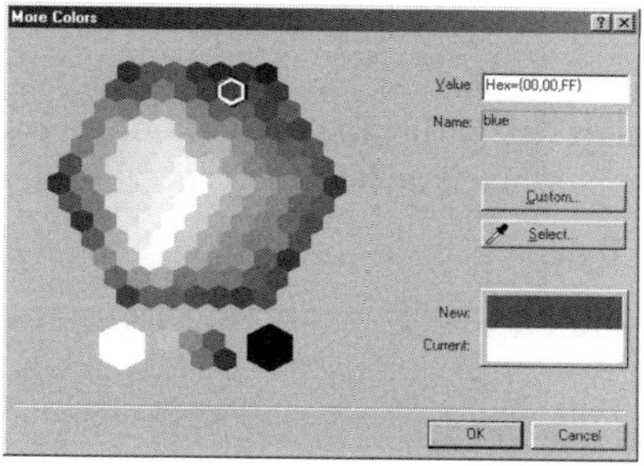

Figure 6.6 Selecting the colour which is closer to the one you require.

3. If you want to define the colour, click on the **Custom** button (see Figure 6.7). Modify the Red, Green and Blue percentage values or modify the **H**, **S** and **L** percentage values. Click on **OK** to confirm.

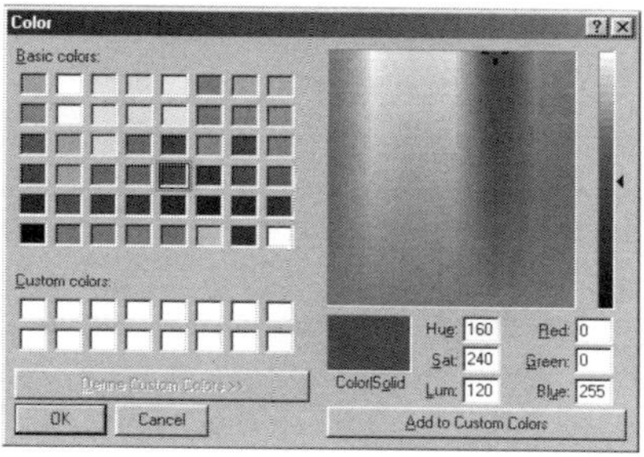

Figure 6.7 You can create your dream colour by defining RGB or HSL percentage values.

FrontPage 2000

4. Another solution is to lift a colour from an image, a text, and so on, in order to define the same colour as a custom colour. To do this, after having displayed the relevant image or text, click on the **Select** button in the **More Colors** dialog box. The pointer changes to a pipette. In the page, click on the colour to be lifted: this is now added to the colour list. Click on **OK** to confirm.

The Font dialog box

To save time whilst formatting, you can use the Font dialog box which groups all the character formatting types.

To open the Font dialog box:

1. After selecting the relevant text, click on **Format, Font** (see Figure 6.8).

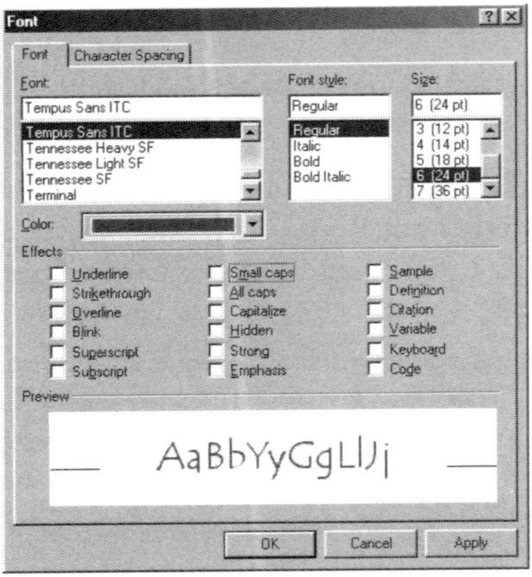

Figure 6.8 With a few clicks, the Font dialog box allows you to define all the character format options.

2. Define your choices, bearing in mind that:
   - The **Font** tab contains all character formats such as attributes (bold, italic, underlined), colour, size, font, and so on.
   - The **Character Spacing** tab allows you to modify spacing between characters as well as the exact position of the text.
3. Click on **OK** to confirm.

■ Formatting paragraphs

A paragraph is a set of characters which ends with a carriage return.

Formatting paragraphs means assigning paragraphs a place on the page, defining spaces before and after them, and so on. A Web page must be perfectly readable and clear.

To delete formatting for a paragraph, select the paragraph, then click on the relevant button to be deactivated in the Format toolbar.

Modification of alignment

Paragraph alignment defines the position of the paragraph in the page. It can begin on the left or on the right of the page, can be centred, and so on. Refer to Figure 6.9 to view each type of alignment. The Format toolbar offers three icons which let you modify alignment. In the default setting, paragraphs are left aligned.

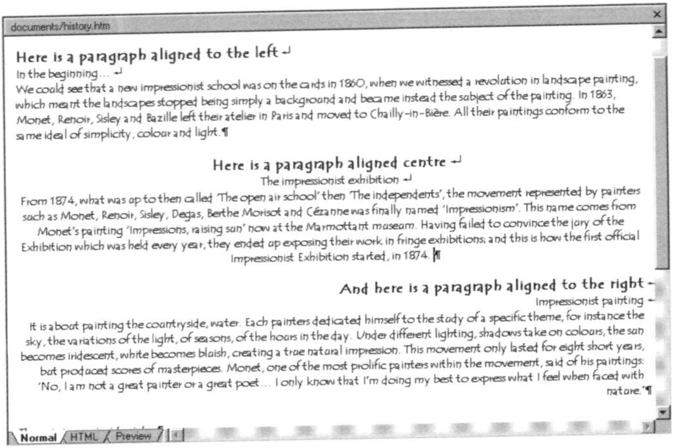

FrontPage 2000

Figure 6.9 The various alignments offered by FrontPage.

To modify paragraph alignment, select the relevant paragraph, then click on the icon which corresponds to what you wish to achieve in the **Format** toolbar: **Left align**, **Centre** and **Right align**.

In our site, centre titles on all pages.

Creation and modification of indents

A paragraph indent consists in leaving a space between the start of a paragraph and the page left margin. FrontPage provides two icons to create and modify paragraph indents.

To create a paragraph indent:

1. Select the relevant paragraph.
2. Click on the **Indents** icon in the **Format** toolbar.

Paragraph dialog box

To save time when formatting paragraphs, you can use the Paragraph dialog box which groups all formatting types.

To open the Paragraph dialog box:

1. After selecting the relevant paragraph, click on **Format, Paragraph** (see Figure 6.10).

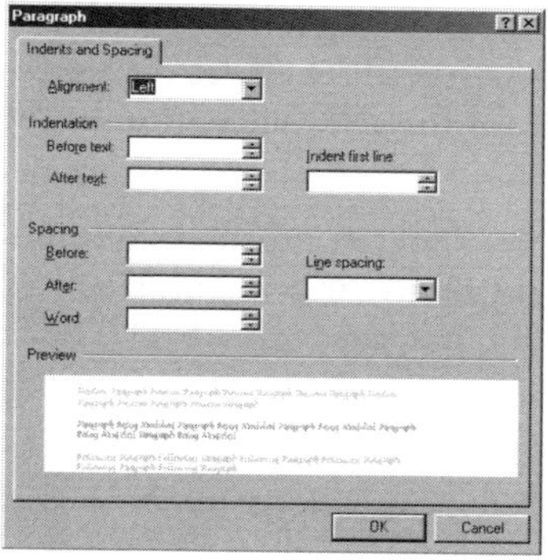

Figure 6.10 With a few clicks, the Paragraph dialog box allows you to define all the formatting options for the paragraph.

2. Define your choice, bearing in mind that:

    - The **Alignment** option allows you to select the alignment you require.
    - The **Indentation** box allows you to define exactly the amount of indentation you wish to apply.
    - The **Spacing** box allows you to define the space to be placed before and after the selected paragraph. The **Line spacing** option allows you to modify spacing between lines in the paragraph.

3. Click on **OK** to confirm.

Bulleted and numbered lists

Bulleted lists allows you to sort text by preceding it with of a number or a bullet (a graphic symbol).

To create a bulleted list quickly, use the **Bullets** and **Numbering** icons available in the Format toolbar. When you click on one of these buttons, FrontPage inserts a number or a bullet. Whenever you enter an element in the list, simply press the **Enter** key to display the next number or a new bullet. When you have finished entering the bulleted list, press on the **Backspace** key or click on the relevant button in the Format toolbar to deactivate it.

In our site, in the Index page, select the contents of the summary (**History, Their best works of art**, and so on). Click on the **Bullets** icon in the Format toolbar (see Figure 6.11). Click outside the selection.

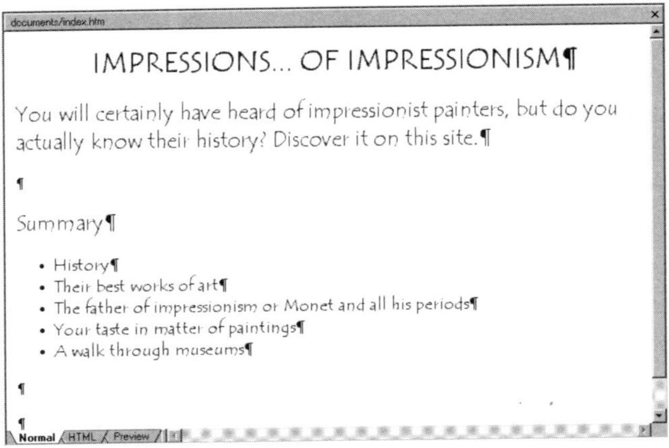

Figure 6.11 The contents of the Summary is now a bulleted list.

The text is displayed as indented with a small round dot before each element.

6: Text: formatting

Modifying bullets and numbers

You can modify the bullets, or the types of number, displayed in the bulleted list:

1. Right click on the bulleted list and select **List Properties** from the menu list (see Figure 6.12).

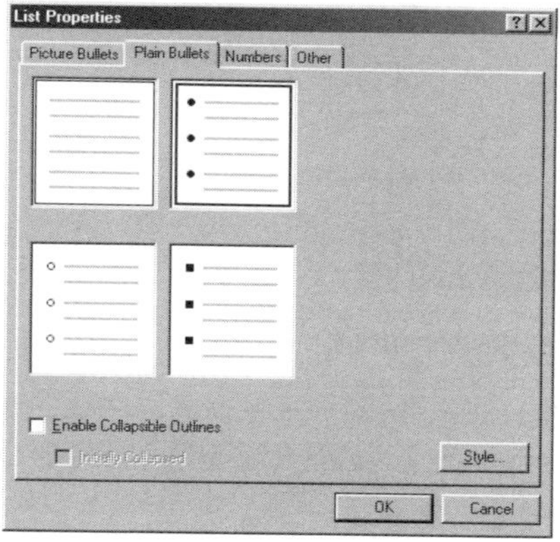

Figure 6.12 You can modify default bullets in FrontPage.

The active Bullets is surrounded by a black box.

2. Click on **Bullets** to activate other available choices. To modify size, colour, and so on for the active bullet, click on the **Style** button, then on the **Format** button in the **Modify Style** dialog box. Define your choice and click on **OK** to confirm.

3. If you want to display a different type of bullet, click on the **Picture Bullets** tab (see Figure 6.13). Click on the **Specify picture** option to activate it, then on the **Browse** button to select the image you wish to apply as a bullet. You can insert a ClipArt image (see Chapter 7). Click on **OK** to confirm.

The defined bullet is displayed in the page.

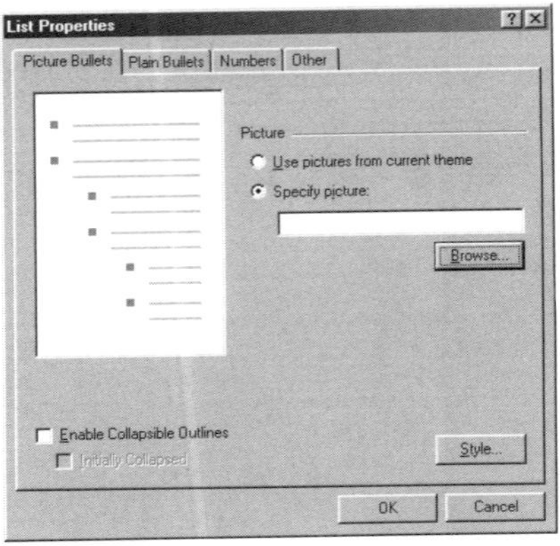

FrontPage 2000

Figure 6.13 You can display any graphic symbol.

For our site, display bullets in yellow.

■ Borders and Shading

The **Borders and Shading** functions allow you to apply a border and a background colour to a paragraph.

Applying a border to a paragraph

If you apply a border to a paragraph, you will give it more prominence. This may be useful when you wish to highlight an important passage.

To create a border for a paragraph:

1. After selecting the paragraph to which you will apply a border, click on **Format, Borders and Shading**. Click on the **Borders** tab (see Figure 6.14).

   Since there is no active border selected at the moment, the border will be the default type.

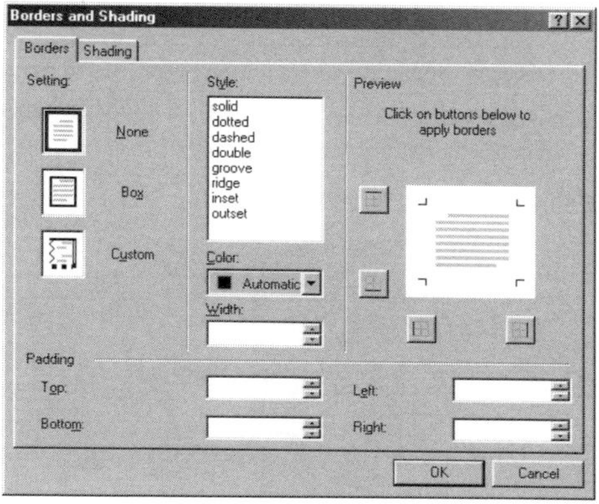

6: Text: formatting

Figure 6.14 The Borders tab in the Borders and Shading dialog box lets you create a border around a paragraph.

2. Click on the **Box** option to create a border. Choose the border style in the relevant option, then the colour. Define margins. Click on **OK** (see Figure 6.15).

> You will certainly have heard of impressionist painters, but do you actually know their history? Discover it on this site.¶

Figure 6.15 Example of a border.

*To delete a border, click on **Format**, **Borders and Shading**. Click on the **Borders** tab, then select **None** in the border settings. Click on **OK** to confirm.*

Paragraph shading

If you apply shading to a paragraph, you create the same highlighting effect as with a border, but the shading looks less 'heavy' on the screen.

FrontPage 2000

To create the background of a paragraph:

1. After selecting the paragraph to which you wish to apply a background, click on **Format, Borders and Shading**. Click on the **Shading** tab (see Figure 6.16).

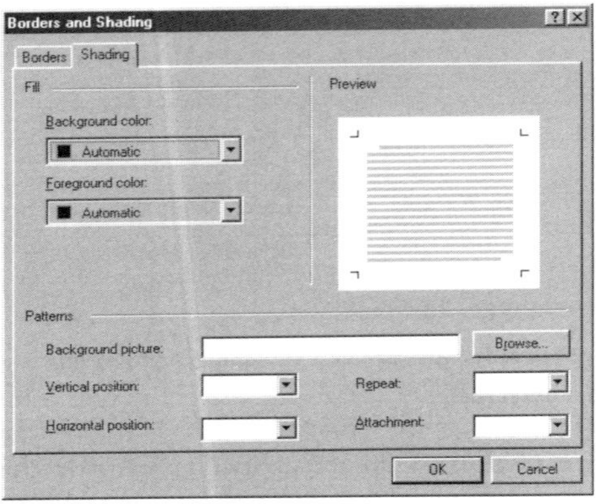

Figure 6.16 Applying shading to a paragraph means assigning a colour to its background.

Since there is no active shading selected at the moment, the background will be the default type.

2. Define the colours. If you want to create a background pattern, click on the **Browse** button, then select the image you require. When you have finished, click on **OK**.

In our site, apply a blue background to all the titles (blue is the default colour).

6: Text: formatting

■ Format painting

In the version 2000 of FrontPage, you can quickly reproduce your format, as you can do in all the other Office applications, using the Format Painter.

To copy formatting:

1. Click on the paragraph or on the text whose format you wish to copy.

   The cursor starts to blink.

2. Click on the **Format Painter** icon in the paragraph and then on the text onto which you want to copy the format.

7 Pictures: inserting and formatting

Inserting pictures
Web images
Formatting pictures

You will learn here how to insert pictures on the Web pages, modify them, and format them in relation to the text.

■ Inserting pictures

For your site to be read, it must be attractive. Of course, you are not forced to add pictures to it, but if you surf the Web, you will notice that most sites do have images.

Pictures add meaning to the rest of the page. They provide more flexibility and can be used as hyperlinks (reactive image).

FrontPage designates as an image anything which is in a graphic format.

Pictures can be:

- pictures from Clip Art;
- pictures from the Web;
- formatting elements such as horizontal lines;
- command buttons;
- scanned pictures.

Clip Art images

Clip Art is the easiest way to add pictures to a page. When you install Office, a Clip Art subfolder is created. The Clip Art Gallery offers a large number of pictures, classified by topic.

To insert a Clip Art image:

1. Position your cursor where you would like to insert the image.
2. Click on **Insert, Picture, Clip Art** (see Figure 7.1).

   The central area displays the various available categories.

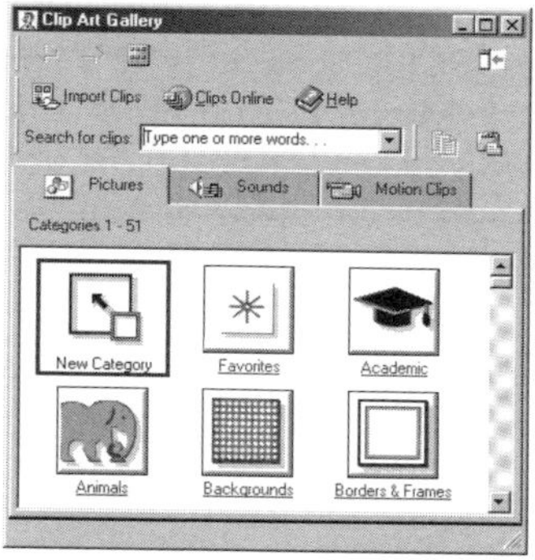

7: Pictures: inserting and formatting

Figure 7.1 The Clip Art Gallery lets you insert pictures in a page of your site.

3. Click on your chosen category (see Figure 7.2). To insert an image, you can either click on it, then on **Insert clip**, or drag it onto the page. If you wish to view the image in a bigger format before inserting it, click on it, then click on **Preview clip**. To view a new category, click on the **Previous** icon in the Clip Art Gallery toolbar.

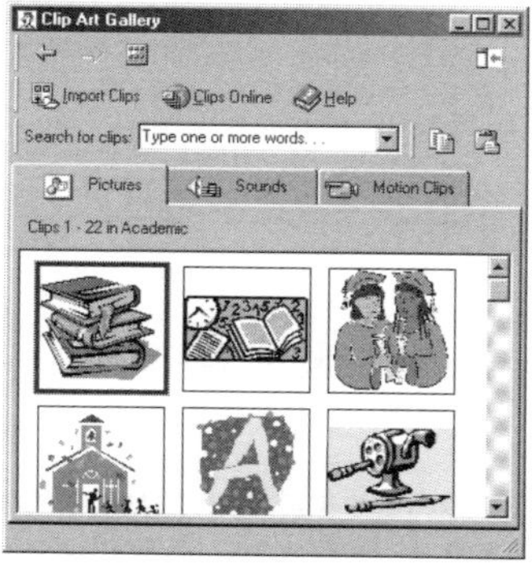

Figure 7.2 Each category offers a number of pictures relating to a topic: music, sport, nature and so on.

FrontPage 2000

4. When you have finished inserting images, you can either close Clip Art by clicking on the **Close** icon in its Title bar, or reduce it by clicking on the **Minimize** icon in its Title bar. In practice, in Office 2000, you can leave Clip Art permanently open in order to access it very quickly.

Finding a Clip Art image

FrontPage 2000 allows us to find a Clip Art image quickly by executing a targeted search.

To find a Clip Art image:

1. After opening the Clip Art Gallery, type the search criteria (word, description, and so on) in the **Search for clips** text box option, then press the **Enter** key.

   The search result is then displayed (see Figure 7.3).

Figure 7.3 The Clip Art search function is very simple. The result is displayed in the central area.

2. Now simply insert the image following the procedures explained in the previous section. If you want to refine the search, click on the image and select **Find clips with similar** in the context menu (see Figure 7.4). Define the words to be selected, the colour, the shape, and so on. The result is displayed next to the first image.

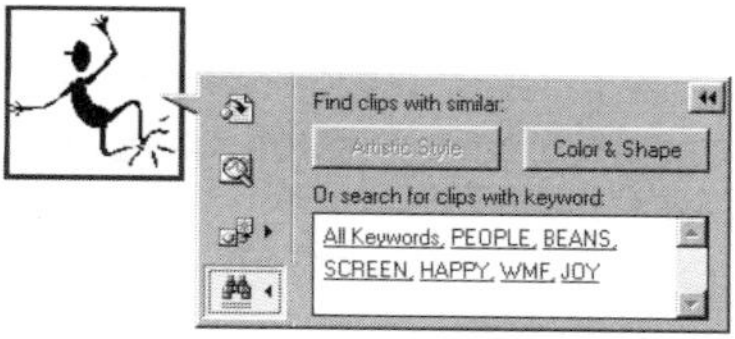

7: Pictures: inserting and formatting

Figure 7.4 Refining the search for pictures.

The Clip Art dialog box offers two additional tabs, as well as the Images tab that we have just seen:

- **Sounds**. Allows you to set up your own sound library.
- **Motion Clips**. Allows you to set up your own video clips library.

Establishing a picture library

If you wish to set up your own picture library, you must import the pictures from other files.

To import pictures:

1. In the **Clip Art Gallery**, in the **Images** tab, click on the **Import Clips** icon (see Figure 7.5).

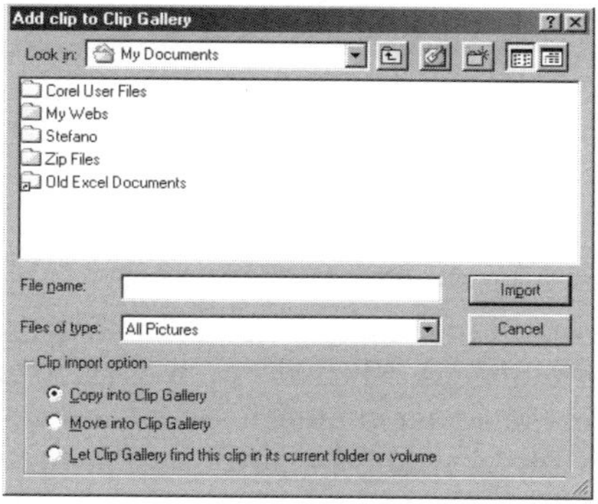

Figure 7.5 The Import clip to Clip Gallery dialog box allows you to select the pictures to be imported.

FrontPage 2000

2. Enter the name of the clip to be inserted in the relevant option. You can also navigate through folders with the traditional procedures. Check the import option to be activated. Click on **Import** (see Figure 7.6).

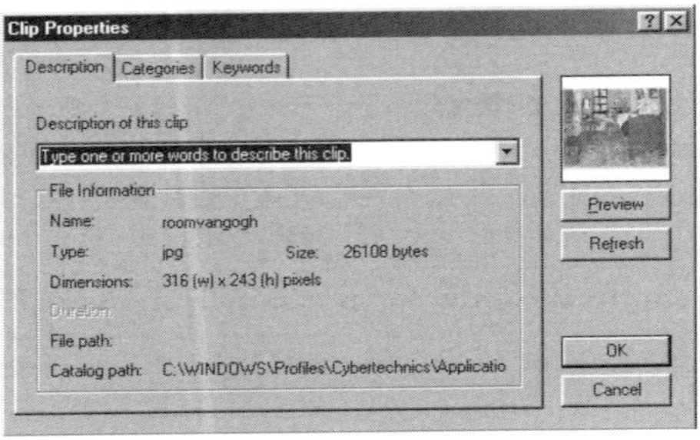

Figure 7.6 The Clip Properties dialog box lets you specify the category into which you wish to insert this clip.

3. Choose a name for the clip. Click on the **Category** tab, then check the category into which you wish to place the image. Assign a keyword to the image. Click on **OK**. Close **Clip Art Gallery**.

Inserting a picture file

You can insert pictures stored on your hard disk in the page for your site.

To insert a picture file:

1. Click on **Insert, Picture, From File** (see Figure 7.7).
2. To insert an image stored in the Image folder, double-click on it in the central area, then double-click on the image to be inserted. To insert an image stored in other folders, click on the **Select a file on your computer** icon (with a magnifying glass and a folder icon). In the dialog box which is displayed, select the folder, then double-click on the image. Click on **OK** to confirm.

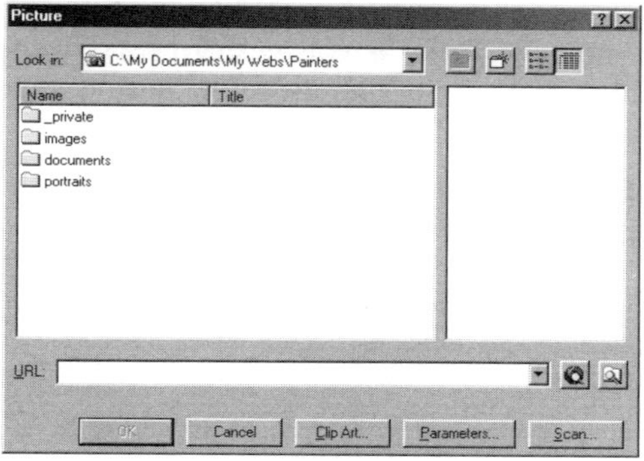

7: Pictures: inserting and formatting

Figure 7.7 The Image dialog box allows you to find an image saved on your hard disk.

Saving images

When you have inserted pictures in the pages for your site, you need to save them:

1. In the page for the relevant site, click on the **Save** icon in the Standard toolbar (see Figure 7.8).

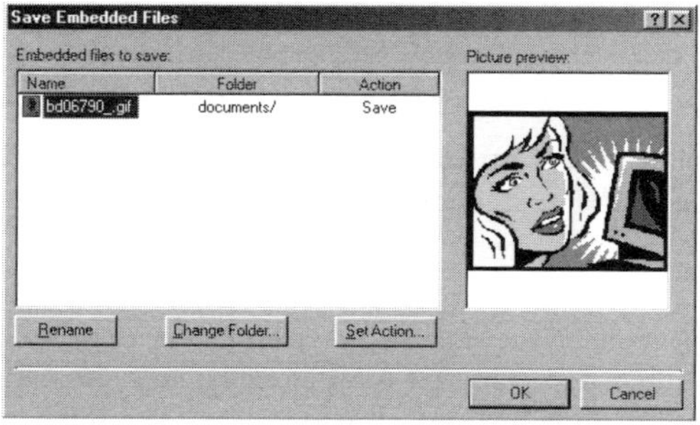

Figure 7.8 You must save the pictures you have inserted.

The pictures that you have inserted are displayed in the central area.

FrontPage 2000

2. To rename an image, click on it, then click on the **Rename** button. Enter the new name. If you wish to modify the destination folder, click on the **Change folder** button, then select the required folder. Click on **OK** to confirm.

The picture files that you have just inserted are displayed in the folder containing the page where you have placed the image.

When you save your files, their name must not exceed eight characters (excluding the extension).

Saving extensions

Pictures are saved in electronic files, with various structures. Each save structure allows you to decode the format in which these pictures were saved.

The two FrontPage save formats are .GIF and .JPEG.

There are other formats, such as .BMP (very frequent under Windows) and .PICT (very frequent under Macintosh), but browsers are unable to decode these types of file. This is why FrontPage Editor automatically converts pictures to .GIF or .JPEG format.

Deleting images

If you decide not to insert an image in the page of your site after all, you need to delete it: click on it and press the **Del** key.

■ Web images

The Web displays a multitude of pictures. You can retrieve these pictures and use them in a page of your site. However, ethically speaking, you should ask the site author for authorisation (unless the image is public domain) and suggest a hyperlink to the site from where you retrieved it.

7: Pictures: inserting and formatting

Retrieving pictures on the Web

To navigate on the Web, you must launch the browser. Once on the Web, display the Web page containing the image, then save it:

1. In the browser, right click on the relevant image.
2. **Select Save Picture**. Click on the arrow of the **Save In** area and select the folder in which you are going to save the image. Enter the file name (less than eight characters). Click on **Save**.
3. Click on **File, Quit** to close the browser.

For anything concerning the creation of our site, go to Pearson Media Group Web site at http://www.pearsoned-ema.com, then save all the pictures on your hard disk.

Save pictures in normal size only, not as thumbnails.

■ Formatting images

When you have inserted the images, you can resize them, colour them, add text to them, and so on.

Resizing an image

For the creation of our site, insert the picture of the **rose** between the words 'really' and 'their', in the first paragraph of the Index page.

The simplest procedure for resizing an image is to click on it, then click on the resizing box in the corner and drag it until you achieve the required size.

There is another, more accurate procedure:

1. In the page, click on the image to be modified. In our example, click on the **rose**.

FrontPage 2000

The image becomes framed by little black dots, which confirms that it is selected.

2. Right click and select **Picture Properties**. Click on the **Appearance** tab (see Figure 7.9).

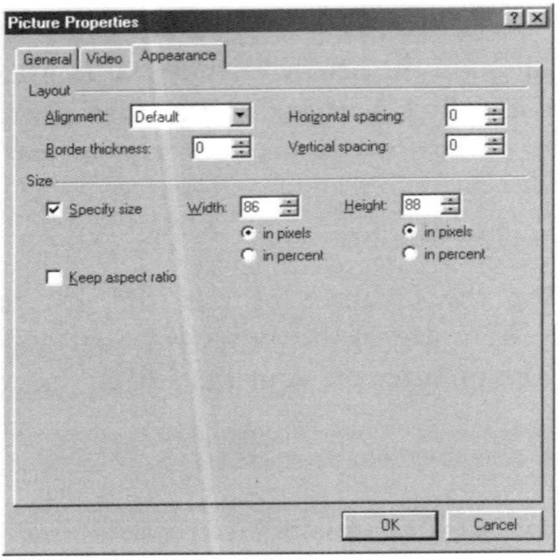

Figure 7.9 The Appearance tab in the Picture properties dialog box lets you modify the size of an image, as well as other features.

3. The Layout zone allows you to specify the exact position for placing the image in relation to the text, define the space before and after the image as well as the thickness of the border around it. Click on the **Specify size** option to activate it. If required, click on the **Keep aspect ratio** option. Double-click on the text box of the **Width** option and type 120. Click on **OK**. Save the image and page.

Placing an image in relation to the text

To place an image accurately in relation to the text:

1. In the page, click on the image to be modified. In our example, click on the **rose**.

7: Pictures: inserting and formatting

2. Click on **Format, Position** (see Figure 7.10). In the **Wrapping Style** area, click on the **Right** option. The **Location and size** box allows you to define, to the nearest pixel, the position of the image in **Width, Height, Left** and **Right** options. Click on **OK** (see Figure 7.11).

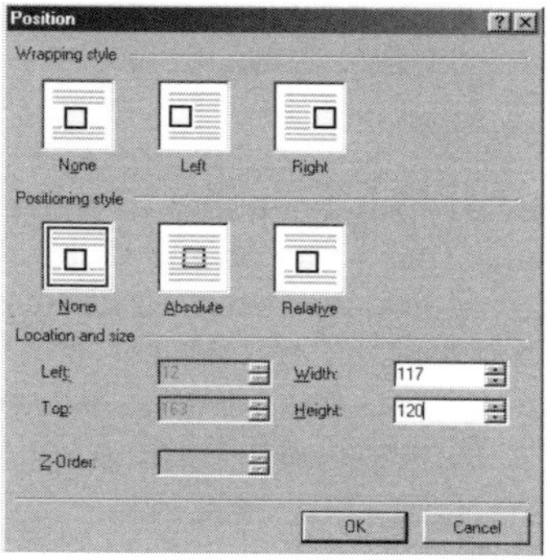

Figure 7.10 The Position dialog box lets you specify the place of the image.

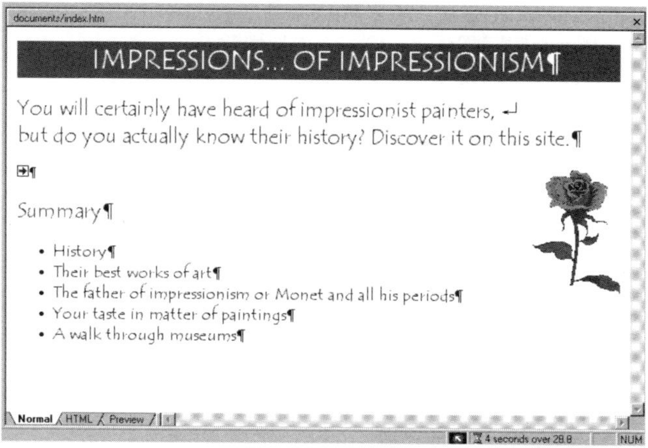

Figure 7.11 The Start Page after formatting the rose picture.

113

FrontPage 2000

Creating a thumbnail

If you find that the image you have just placed is too large, you might want to create a thumbnail version. The **autothumbnail** function is very practical and easy to use, because it allows you to display the image at minimum size in the Web page, then, when you click on it, the picture can be viewed in its normal size.

To create the thumbnail for an image:

1. The Monet page will contain a certain number of paintings by this Grand Master. In order to avoid the pictures taking up too much space, it would be better to change them all to thumbnails. Therefore, in the Monet page, insert the following paintings in this order, **Monet seascapes**, **Monet waterlilies**, **Monet beaches** and **Monet harbour** views.

2. Click on one picture, then on the **Create thumbnail** icon in the Pictures toolbar (see Figure 7.12). Save the modifications. Repeat the same procedure in order to insert all the painters' portraits in the **History** page, next to their name (see Figure 7.13).

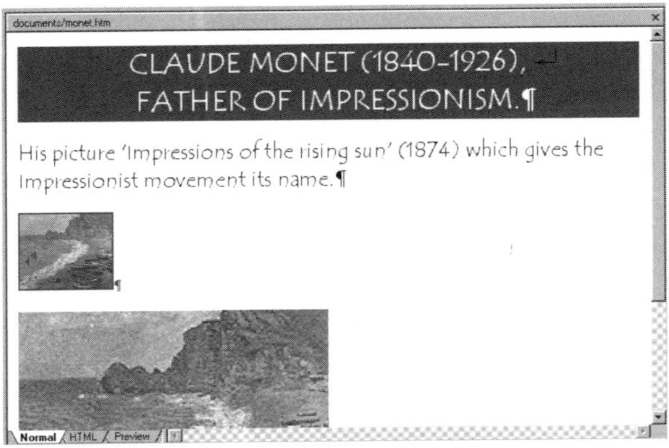

Figure 7.12 The pictures are now thumbnails.

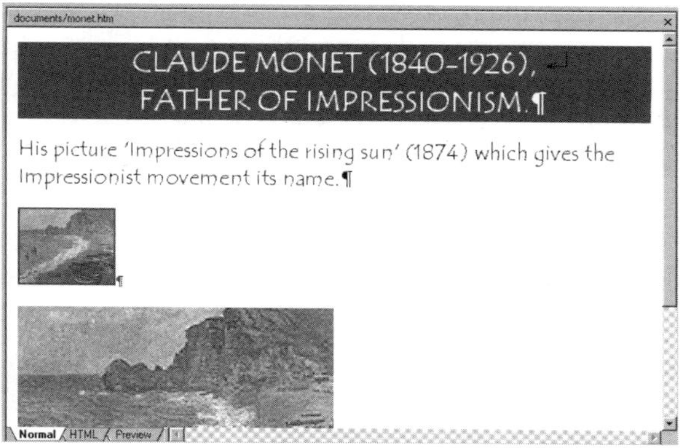

7: Pictures: inserting and formatting

Figure 7.13 The History page after inserting their paintings, changed to thumbnails. Simply click on them to view them in normal size.

By default, thumbnails have a 50 pixels width, but you can easily modify this parameter.

To modify thumbnail size and border:

1. Click on **Tools**, **Page Options**, then click on the **Autothumbnail** tab (see Figure 7.14).

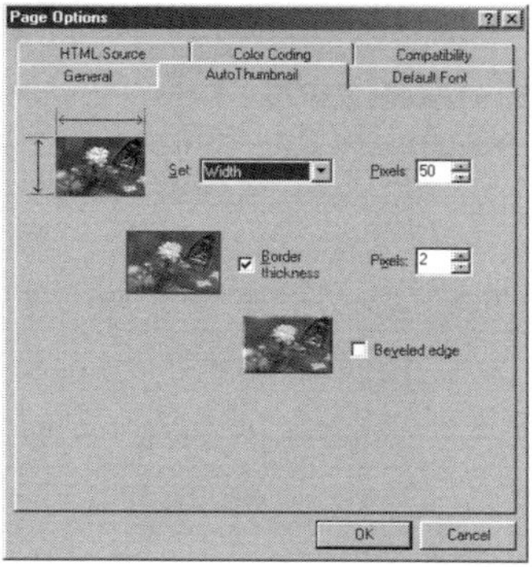

Figure 7.14 Define size and border for the thumbnails you create.

115

2. Define the size, the thickness of the border and, if you so wish, the raised border. Click on **OK**.

Thumbnail modifications do not apply to those which have already been created.

Inserting text into a picture

You can insert text into a picture in order to make it clearer or more attractive:

1. Select the relevant image, then click on the **Text** icon in the Pictures toolbar.

   A frame is displayed with the cursor flashing.

2. Enter the text you want. If you wish to format your text in any way, select it, then apply the formats we have learnt in the previous chapter.

*To delete a text in a picture, click on it, then press the **Del** key.*

Pictures Toolbar

You have no doubt noticed that when you select a picture, a specific toolbar is displayed. This is the **Pictures** toolbar which contains a number of icons for modifying, moving or colouring the selected picture. Here is a description of the icons in this toolbar which we will not be using in this chapter.

7: Pictures: inserting and formatting

Icon	Function
	Lets you insert a picture within a file.
	Lets you place the picture in relation to the text.
	When several pictures are 'stacked' one on top of the other, lets you move a picture up or down within the stack.
	Lets you rotate the picture.
	Lets you increase or decrease brightness and contrast.
	Allows you to crop a picture.
	Allows you to change a colour to transparent.
	Allows you to change the picture to black and white, to clean it up, to make it three-dimensional and to create a sample.
	Once activated, marks the selected image.
	Allows you to insert an interactive area in the picture and underline it.
	Allows you to restore the picture to its original aspect before saving.

117

FrontPage 2000

Site continuity

Insert all the pictures, place them and format them the same way as they appear in Pearson site, at **http://www.pearsoned-ema.com**.

In the next chapter, you will display a coloured background. For the rose (which has a grey background) not to appear with an empty background, you must make it transparent.

To do this, click on the rose, then click on the **Set Transparent Colour** icon in the Pictures toolbar. Do not forget to save it.

8
Advanced formatting and Help tools

Themes
Formatting pages
Text animation
Finding and replacing text
Spelling

FrontPage 2000

If you have followed our procedures, your site is already substantially developed. In this chapter, you will learn about more complex formatting options than simply creating a background, framing a page, and so on. You will also be shown how to make your site truly perfect by making sure that its spelling is faultless.

■ Themes

There are about sixty new themes in FrontPage 2000. Choosing a theme is the ideal method to apply a quick 'one-stop' format to your site. Use this when you must produce a site quickly or when you cannot create a customised format.

To apply a topic to a site:

1. After opening the site, in the Page view, click on **Format, Theme** (see Figure 8.1).

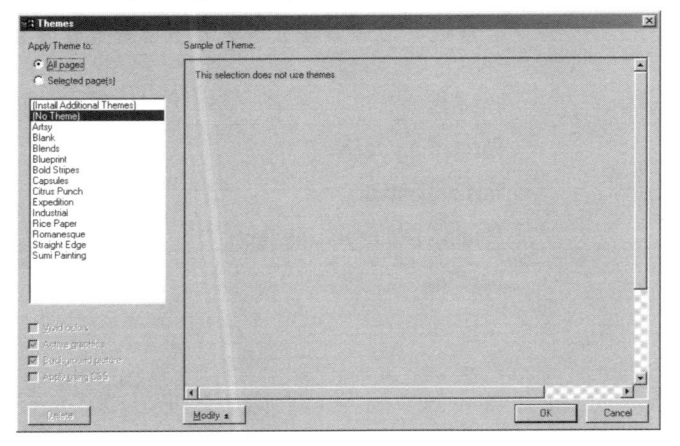

Figure 8.1 The Themes dialog box lets you view the set of themes available in FrontPage.

8: Advanced formatting and Help tools

2. The various themes are displayed in the list on the left. Clicking on one of the themes lets you preview its style in the **Sample of Theme** area of the dialog box. Click on the theme you want to use.

3. At the bottom of the theme list there are options which let you define the theme application mode with a high degree of accuracy. For example, you can choose to use vivid colours or to display a background picture. Make your choice, then click on **OK** to apply the theme to your site.

To apply a theme to a single page:

1. After opening the page in Page view, click on **Format**, then on **Theme**.

2. Select the theme to be applied, define the options, then click on the **Selected pages** option. Now simply click on **OK** to apply the theme to your page.

■ Formatting pages

FrontPage offers commands to frame the whole text in a page, display a background in colour or a picture, and so on.

Framing all text in a page

Since we have dealt with this procedure only very briefly earlier on in Chapter 6, we will return to it, but not in great detail.

To create a border around all paragraphs:

1. After selecting the whole page, click on **Format, Borders and Shading,** then on the **Borders** tab (see Figure 8.2).

2. Click on the **Box** option to create a frame. Choose the style in the relevant option, then the colour. Define the margins. Click on **OK**.

FrontPage 2000

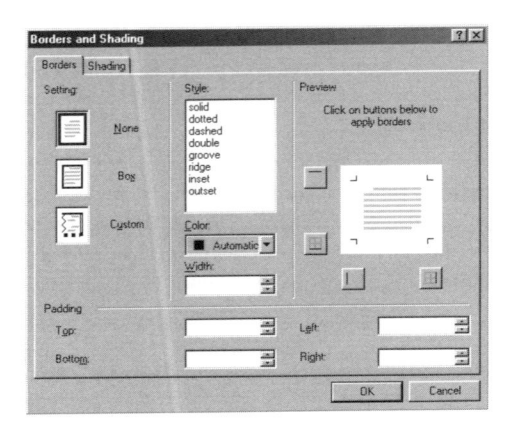

Figure 8.2 You can define the border type you wish to apply in the Borders and Shading dialog box.

> To delete all borders from a page, select the relevant page, click on **Format, Borders and Shading**. Click the **Borders** tab, select **None** from the setting options. Click **OK** to confirm.

Page background

When you apply a background to a page, you emphasise it in the same way as with a frame, but the background appears less 'heavy' on the screen.

To create the background for all text in a page:

1. After selecting the page you wish to create a background for, click on **Format, Borders and Shading**. Click on the **Shading** tab (see Figure 8.3).
2. Define the foreground and background colours. If you wish to create a pattern for the background, click on the **Browse** button, then select the required image. When you have finished, click on **OK**.

122

8: Advanced formatting and Help tools

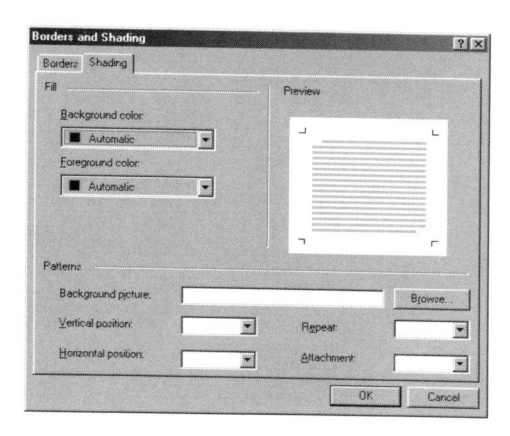

Figure 8.3 Creating a background for a page means displaying a coloured background for all the text in that page.

Coloured background

Let's apply a coloured background to your pages. You do not have to do this, however, bearing in mind that a page should be readable. Choose a dark blue background for our site.

To apply a coloured background to a page:

1. In our site, open the **Index** page in the Page view. Click on **Format, Background** (see Figure 8.4). Alternatively, right click on the page and select **Page Properties**. Click on the **Background** tab.

2. In the **Colors** area, click on the arrow in the **Background** option, then on the colour swatch you want to give the background. In our example, click on **More colors** (see Figure 8.5). Click on the fourth swatch from the top left, which is blue. Click on **OK** to confirm, then on **OK** to close the **Page Properties** dialog box.

The page background is now deep blue (see Figure 8.6).

FrontPage 2000

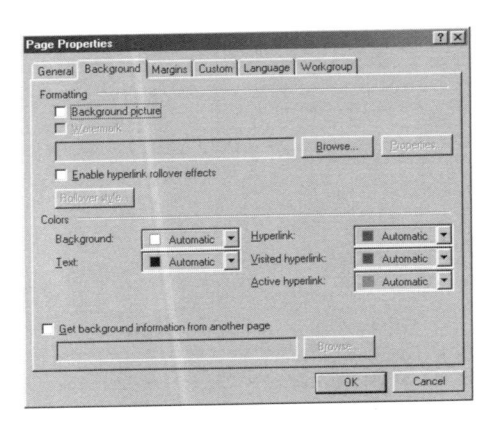

Figure 8.4 This is the dialog box that lets you choose a background.

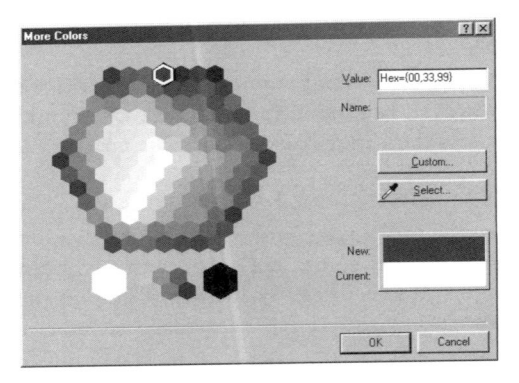

Figure 8.5 Choose a lovely blue background colour.

> *To set the text colour of your site, and so that all new text is inserted in the same colour as the rest of the text, in the **Background** tab click on the arrow in the **Text** option and select the text colour. Click on **OK** to confirm.*

124

8: Advanced formatting and Help tools

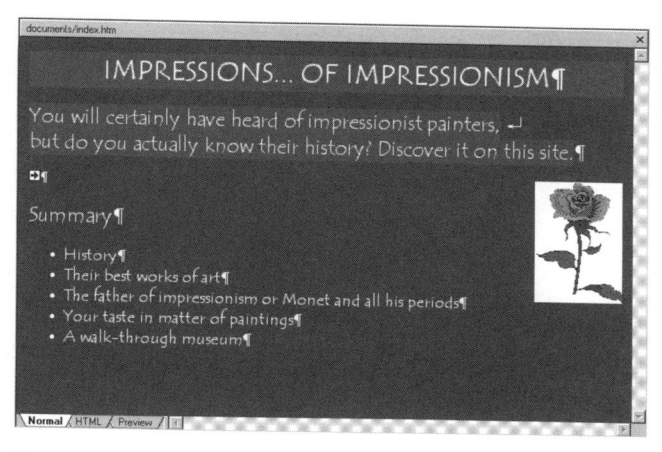

Figure 8.6 You have just created a blue background. This is without doubt the most appropriate colour to bring out the best in the lighting effects used in impressionist painting.

*To delete a background, open the **Page Properties** dialog box, **Background** tab. Click the arrow in the **Background** option in the **Colors** area and select **Automatic**. Click on **OK** to confirm.*

Apply the background from another page

To avoid having to repeat the same formatting operations for each page in your site, let us now see how we can apply another page's background to a page in the same site:

1. Display the required page in the Page view. In our site, open the History page. Click on Format, Background.
2. Select the Get background information from another page option. Click the Browse button (see Figure 8.7). Select the folder containing the page. In our site, click on documents then on Index. Click OK to confirm, then on OK to close the Page Properties dialog box.

125

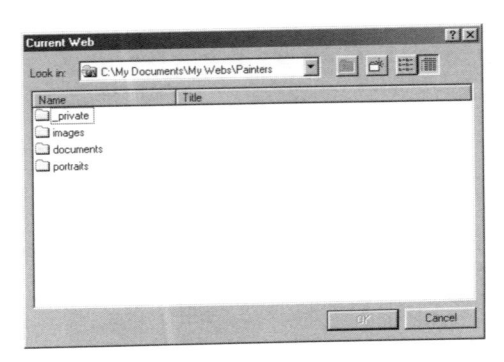

Figure 8.7 You can choose to use a background from another page.

3. Repeat the same procedures for each page in the site. Do not forget to save.

Creating a picture background

If you are not too fond of your coloured background, you can choose an actual picture as a background for your page. You need to be aware that the chosen picture will not be displayed as a whole throughout the page, but it will appear as a stepped-up mosaic of the same picture.

To create a picture background:

1. Display the page in Page view. Click on **Format, Background**. Check the **Background picture** option. Click on the **Browse** button (see Figure 8.8).

2. To choose a picture stored in the site, use the central area. To choose a Clip Art picture, click on the **Clip Art** button. To choose a picture stored on your hard disk, click on the **Select file on your computer** icon (the magnifying glass and the folder). To search for a picture on the Web, click on the **Use your Web browser** icon (the magnifying glass and the earth globe). Once you have chosen, click on **OK** to confirm, then on **OK** to close the **Page Properties** dialog box.

8: Advanced formatting and Help tools

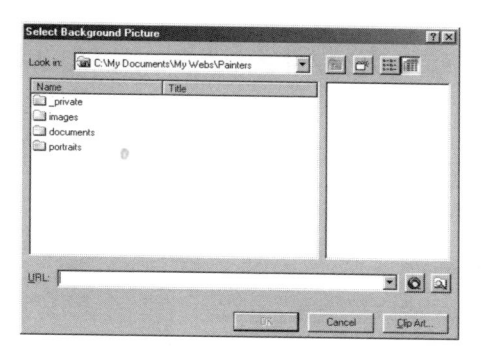

Figure 8.8 Finding a picture to display as a background to your page.

Splitting paragraphs

When you type text, the line break is decided automatically by the software. To make a line break, you must press the Enter key: a new paragraph is then started.

When you have created a paragraph, you can split it. For example, in the Monet title page the title is probably too long, so it would be better to split it.

To split the paragraph, point just in front of '**The father of impressionism**' text, click, then press the **Shift** key: the paragraph is split into two, without creating a new paragraph.

Inserting lines

Inserting lines can often be useful when formatting your page. In this way, you will add some visual space to your text.

1. Display the relevant page in the **Page** view.
2. Bring the cursor to where you wish to insert the line. Click on **Insert, Horizontal line**.

*To delete a line, click on the line and press the **Del** key.*

Modifying a line

If you want to modify the aspect of a line, its context menu offers a **Modify** dialog box.

To modify a line:

1. Right click on the line to be modified and select **Horizontal Line Properties** (see Figure 8.9).

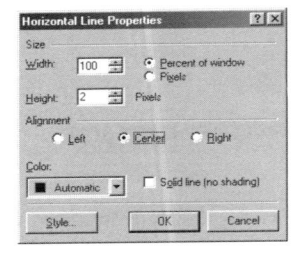

Figure 8.9 You can modify a line using this dialog box.

You can modify the width, the height, the alignment and the colour of your line.

To modify a value, simply click on the arrow next to the relevant option and make your choice.

2. Carry out your modifications. Click on **OK** to confirm.

Copying a line

If you wish the line you have created to be displayed at the end of all paragraphs in your page, you must copy it, then paste where you wish it to appear:

1. Click on the line to be selected, then on **Edit, Copy**.
2. Point to where you wish the line to be copied and click. Click on **Edit, Paste**.

A new line will be displayed.

8: Advanced formatting and Help tools

■ Text animation

As in PowerPoint, you can animate text in your Web pages. These animations are known as DHTML (*Dynamic Hyper-Text Markup Language*). Before applying them to your site, find out if your provider can publish this type of extension.

To create animated text effects:

1. Display the page in the Page view, select the relevant text, then click on **Format, Dynamic HTML Effects**.

   The DHTML Effects toolbar is displayed (see Figure 8.10).

Figure 8.10 The DHTML Effects toolbar allows you to create animation effects for Web pages.

2. You must start by instructing FrontPage as to which 'event' is going to launch the animation. Click on the arrow in the **On** option (see Figure 8.11). Select the required action.

Figure 8.11 You must always define an event to launch the animation.

3. Now, you must define the type of animation. Click on the arrow in the **Apply** option and select the required option, bearing in mind that **Fly out** makes the text 'fly', and that **Formatting** allows you to define multiple formatting and colour options and so on. Now simply choose the animation settings that you like, click on the arrow in the Choose settings option and select your desired setting.

FrontPage 2000

> *To delete a DHTML effect, click on the relevant text, right click on a toolbar, select **DHTML Effects**. Click on **Remove Effect**.*

■ Finding and replacing text

The **Find and Replace** function allows you to search for a word and replace it with another.

1. Display the relevant page in the Page view. Click on **Edit, Replace** (see Figure 8.12).

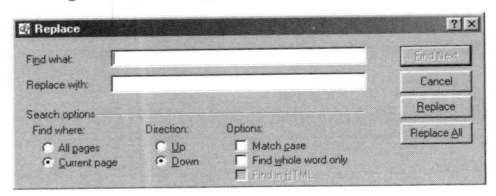

Figure 8.12 The Replace dialog box allows you to select a word that you want to replace over the whole of your page.

2. In the **Find what** option, type the word to be found. In the **Replace with** option, type the new word. Click on **Find Next** to display the first occurrence of the word.

   FrontPage highlights the word you are searching for.

3. Click on **Replace**.

   FrontPage replaces the highlighted word with the new one.

4. Click on **Find Next** so that FrontPage can find if the word also appears elsewhere on the page. Repeat the procedure as many times as necessary.

   When FrontPage can no longer find the word you are searching for, it displays a dialog box letting you know that the search is completed.

5. Click **OK,** then click on the **Close** icon in the Title bar dialog box.

8: Advanced formatting and Help tools

> *In the **Replace** dialog box, you can click on **Replace All** and FrontPage will automatically replace that word with the new word throughout the page.*

■ Spelling

It is paramount that text should be correct. You will loose credibility if you write impressionists with a single 's'! FrontPage offers two functions to ensure that your spelling is spot on.

AutoSpelling

AutoSpelling used to feature in the other Office applications, but not in FrontPage. This has now been put right. You can use AutoSpelling to show you any errors by underlining them with a wavy red line.

To use AutoSpelling, click on **Tools, Page Options**. In the General tab (see Figure 8.13), tick the **Check spelling as you type** option. Click on **OK** to confirm.

Figure 8.13 Tick this option in Page Options to ensure correct spelling.

FrontPage 2000

Once this option is active, all 'errors' will appear underlined in a wavy red line. To correct them:

1. Right click on the wavy red line under the word 'Histor' (see Figure 8.14).

Figure 8.14 The context menu allows errors to be corrected.

2. Correct, bearing in mind that:
   - One or more words are suggested as replacement. Simply click on the one you want and this will automatically replace the original misspelt word.
   - The **Ignore All** option means that this word will no longer be notified as wrong throughout the site.
   - The **Add** option lets you add this word to the FrontPage dictionary so that it will no longer be notified as wrong.

Launching the Spell Checker

If the wavy red lines bother you, you can decide not to spell-check automatically while you are typing. In this case, to make sure that the site is error-free, you must use the Spell Checker function after typing your text.

8: Advanced formatting and Help tools

1. Open a page in the **Page** view. Click on **Tools, Spelling** or press the F7 function key (see Figure 8.15).

Figure 8.15 Spell Checker is now open and indicates a word which it does not recognise.

- The **Not in dictionary** box indicates that the word is not present in the dictionary.
- The **Change To** box displays a correct word that you can modify, either by typing it again, or by clicking on a choice in the **Suggestions** box.

2. While you are carrying out the check, click on:
   - **Ignore**. Allows you to move to the next correction.
   - **Ignore All**. Allows you to move to the next correction and not to have to stop for this 'error' again.
   - **Change**. Allows you to replace the word in the **Not in Dictionary** box with the word in the **Change To** box.
   - **Change All**. Allows you to replace the word not in the dictionary with the word in the **Change To** box, and this throughout the page.
   - **Add**. Lets you add the word to the dictionary in the **Add words to** box.
   - **Suggestions**. Lets you view suggested alternative words in the **Suggestions** list.

3. Click on **OK** to confirm the end of correction message.

9 Frames, tables and multimedia

Frames
Tables
Sound
Video clips
Animated pictures

FrontPage 2000

In this chapter, you will learn how to create a page containing frames and to test your frames in the browser. Then, you will design a table, format it and modify it. To finish, you will learn about FrontPage multimedia functions.

■ Frames

A frame is a navigation window within a page. The contents of this frame can be used and read, independent of the rest of the page. Also, actions in a frame can involve actions in another frame.

A typical application of using frames is the MSN summary (see Figure 9.1).

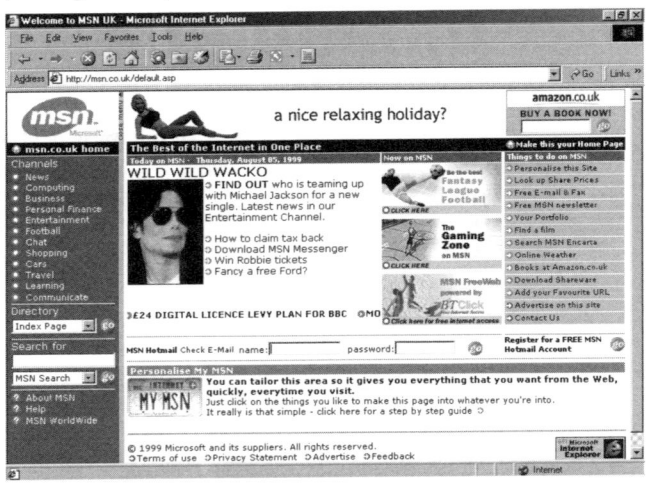

Figure 9.1 This Web page presents its summary in a frame.

The narrower frame on the left is the summary. It contains the list of all pages on this site.

9: Frames, tables and multimedia

Each element in this summary is a hyperlink which takes you to a corresponding page. When you click on a link in this list, the corresponding page is displayed in the larger frame, on the right. Currently, the frame on the right displays the contents of the selected page.

Frames are very interesting: they allow you to go easily and quickly to any page in the site by clicking on the relevant link in the summary.

A Web page can contain as many frames as you want. But be careful, if there are too many of them, they may be too small.

Frames Pages

The term Frames Pages indicates the set of frames in a page. A FrontPage page with frames is a composite of several FrontPage pages with an additional frame containing the properties of the Frames Pages. Each frame is made up as a FrontPage page. A summary could include:

- a first page, containing the Table of Contents frame;
- a second page, containing the Body frame;
- a third page, which allows you to specify the properties for Frames Pages.

Creating Frames Pages

We will see here how to create Frames Pages to set the Table of Contents for a site. Do not worry if you have already created a start page which allows you to access the various pages in your site. With the summary, your visitors will be able to navigate throughout the site without having to return to the start page.

To create Frames Pages:

1. In Page view, click on **File, New, Page**. In the new dialog box, click on the **Frames Pages** tab (see Figure 9.2).

FrontPage 2000

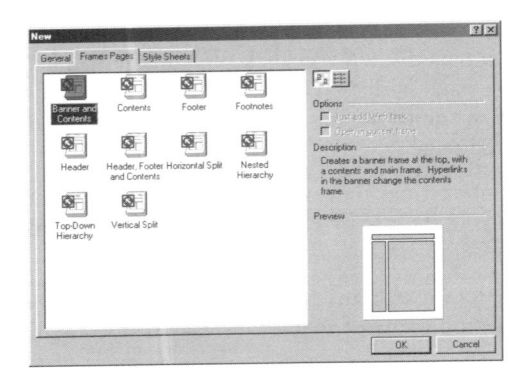

Figure 9.2 This dialog box allows you to choose a template for creating Frames Pages.

2. Click on **Contents** in the list which is displayed. A list with other choices is available. Use it to create **Frames Pages**.
3. Click on **OK** (see Figure 9.3).

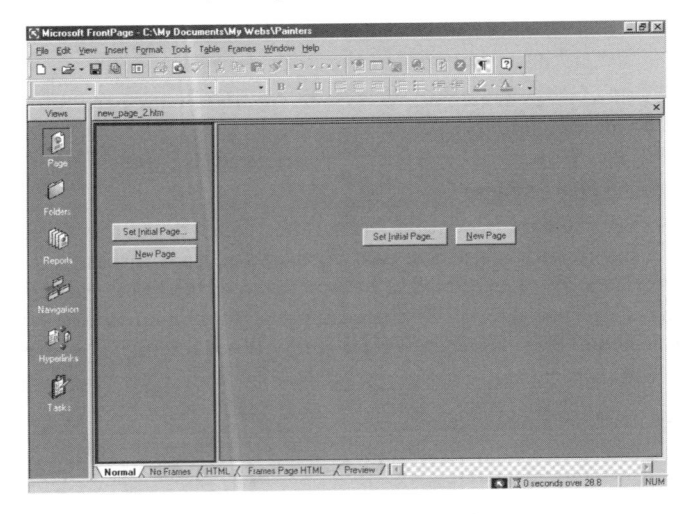

Figure 9.3 The Frames Pages Contents is displayed.

138

9: Frames, tables and multimedia

Creating the first frame

You can either create a new page, or use an existing one. Now, let us see how to create Frames Page:

1. Click on **New Page** in the frame on the left.

   The frame is empty and the pointer flashes (see Figure 9.4).

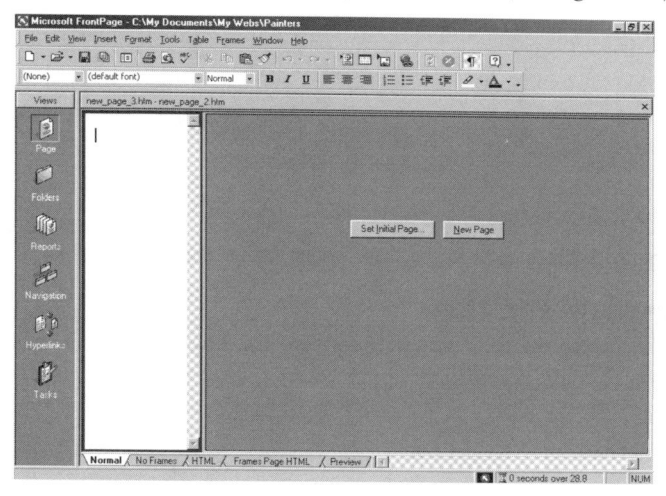

Figure 9.4 A Table of Contents is entered.

2. Enter, for example, the **Table of Contents** of the relevant site. Remember to press the **Enter** key after each item.
3. Apply formats to the **Table of Contents** (font, size, colour).

Using an existing page

As we have just stated, you can use an existing page for your Table of Contents frame.

1. Click on the **Set Initial page** button in the frame on the right (see Figure 9.5).
2. Select the required page and click on **OK** to confirm.

FrontPage 2000

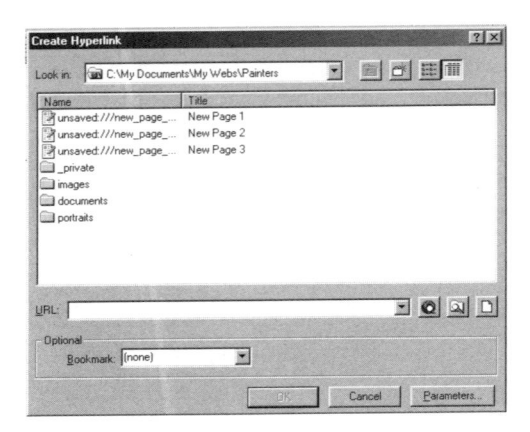

Figure 9.5 Choosing an existing page for the Table of Contents Frames Page.

Creating the second frame

The frame on the right will contain the body page. You can either create a new page, or use an existing one (see the relevant topic).

To create the second frame:

1. Click on **New Page** in the frame.

   The frame is displayed as empty and the pointer flashes.

2. Edit the page as shown in previous chapters.

3. Apply the various formats to the body frame: pictures, characters, font, size, colour, and so on.

Defining the properties for created pages

You must now define the properties for created pages:

1. Right click in the body frame and select **Page Properties** (see Figure 9.6).

2. Fill in the various options. Click on **OK**.

3. Repeat the same procedures for the **Table of Contents**.

9: Frames, tables and multimedia

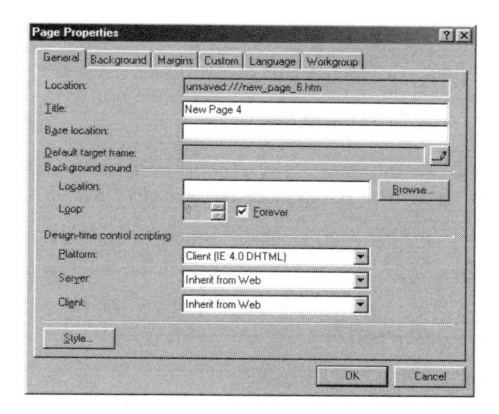

Figure 9.6 Defining page properties.

Defining Frames properties

You must now define the properties for each frame:

1. In the **Table of Contents** frame, right click and select **Frame Properties** (see Figure 9.7).

Figure 9.7 Defining the properties for the first frame.

2. Enter a name. In the **Options** area, select **Show scrollbars** if needed. You can define margins and size of frame.

141

FrontPage 2000

3. Click on **OK**.
4. Repeat the same procedures for the other frames.

Defining Frames Pages

For the link between frames to work, you need to create a third frame containing all the properties of Frames Pages.

1. Right click anywhere in the **Page view** window and select **Frame Properties**.
2. In the dialog box, click on **Frames Page**, then click on the **General** tab (see Figure 9.8).

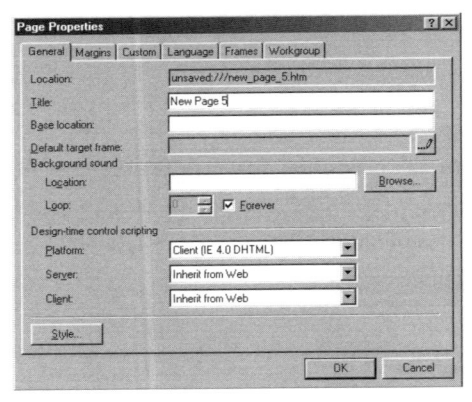

Figure 9.8 The General tab in the Frame Properties dialog box allows you to assign a name to Frame Pages.

3. Fill in the **Title** box. The other tabs let you choose **Frames Page** formats.
4. Click on **OK**, then click on **OK** in the **Page Properties** dialog box to confirm.

9: Frames, tables and multimedia

Saving Frames Pages

When you have finished all your formatting and defining of frames, you must remember to save all your frames. You can do this as follows:

1. Click on **File, Save As**.
2. In the **Save In** box, click on the arrow and select the required folder.
3. Name the **Frames Page** in the **File name** box, then click on **Save**.

   The dialog box closes, then opens again for you to save the first frame.

4. In the **File name** box, the name of your frame is displayed; click on **Save** to confirm.

   The dialog box closes, then opens again for you to save the second frame.

5. In the **File name** box, the name of your frame is displayed; click on **Save** to confirm.

Your Frames Page is now finished. For this page to work, hyperlinks will have to be created between each single item in the table of contents. To do this, you will have to refer back to the chapter describing how to create hyperlinks between the various pages.

Any surfer who will be navigating your site will be able to display the active page in the contents in the frame on the right.

When creating frames, the WYSIWYG principle does not apply. Therefore do not be surprised if you cannot check your hyperlinks in Frames Pages.

Testing Frames Pages

Having established that creating frames in FrontPage does not conform to WYSIWYG principles, it is important that the page be tested in an actual Web browser.

1. To test all the links, click on the **Preview in Browser** icon in the Standard toolbar.
2. In the browser, check all the hyperlinks. Click on **File, Close** to close the browser.

■ Tables

A table allows you to structure data. Information becomes much more meaningful when it is properly sorted. In FrontPage, tables allow you better control in positioning items placed on a page, such as text, form fields or pictures.

The basic element in a table is the cell. A cell is a grid unit which can contain all sorts of data: text, picture, and so on.

A table has a number of properties for configuration purposes, such as number of rows, columns, thickness and coloured borders, background colour or texture, and so on.

Creating a table

You will now create a table with a number of Impressionist paintings. (You will have retrieved these pictures in the previous chapters.) Have a look at the Paintings page and follow the instructions in order to create the same table.

Since creating tables is complicated, FrontPage offers a Tables toolbar. Click on **View, Toolbars, Tables** (see Figure 9.9).

Figure 9.9 The Tables toolbar lets you activate table commands.

9: Frames, tables and multimedia

The actions available in the Tables toolbar are the following:

- **Draw Table**. Inserts a table in the page.
- **Eraser**. Clears cells, Frames, and so on.
- **Insert Rows**. Adds rows to your table.
- **Insert Columns**. Adds columns to your table.
- **Delete Cells**. Deletes cells.
- **Merge Cells**. Merges several cells into a single cell.
- **Split Cells**. Splits one cell into several cells.
- **Align Top**. Aligns the text to the top of the cell.
- **Center Vertically**. Centres text in the cell.
- **Align Bottom**. Aligns text at the bottom of the cell.
- **Distribute Rows Evenly**. Distributes rows evenly.
- **Distribute Columns Evenly**. Distributes columns evenly.
- **Fill Colour**. Selects a coloured background for the table.
- **AutoFit**. Allows you to fit the cell to its text.

To create a table:

1. In our site, open the **Paintings** page. Insert a row between the title and the sentence. Click on **Table, Insert, Table** (see Figure 9.10).

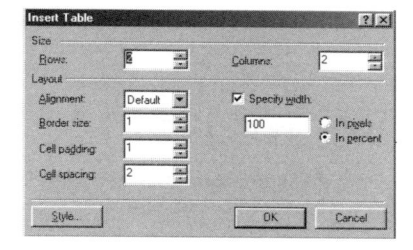

Figure 9.10 The Insert table dialog box is displayed. You must choose the number of columns and rows.

FrontPage 2000

2. In the **Rows** option in the **Size** box, type 9. In the **Columns** option in the **Size** box, type 2. The other options available let you define table alignment and border settings for the table. Click on **OK**.

The table is displayed (see Figure 9.11).

Figure 9.11 The table is displayed as you have defined it.

Entering text in a table

To enter text in a table, click in a cell, then type the text.

To move from one cell to another, use the **Tab** key.

To change row, press the **Tab** key, then press a direction arrow (**up**, **down**, **right**, **left**).

You will now enter text and insert pictures to make the table shown in Figure 9.12. If you need to, follow the example of the same page in the site. Then, apply the Tempus font without ITC in 24-pt to the names of the painters.

9: Frames, tables and multimedia

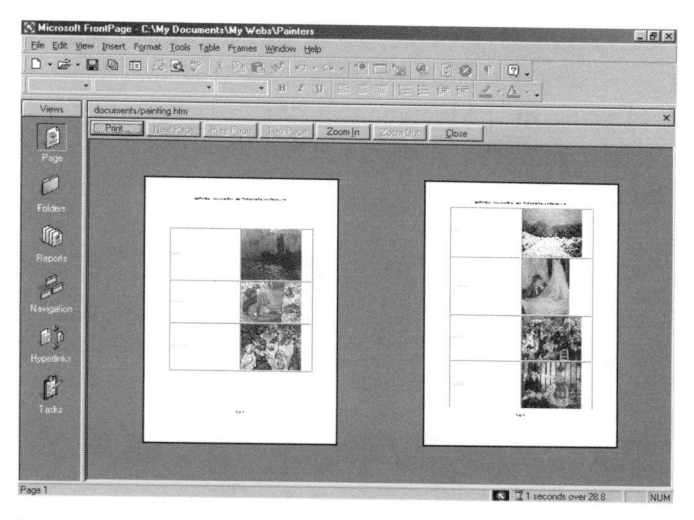

Figure 9.12 The data you will need to enter in the table.

> *When you type the text, remember to activate it in yellow, otherwise you will not be able to see anything!*

To insert a new row at the end of the table, place the cursor at the end of the last row, then press the **Tab** key or click on the **Insert Rows** icon in the **Tables** toolbar.

To insert an extra row in a table, click on where you want the row, then click on the **Insert Rows** icon in the **Tables** toolbar.

To delete a row, place the pointer on the row, click on it to select it, then click on **Table, Delete Cells** or on the **Delete Cells** icon in the Tables toolbar.

Borders

A table always looks better when its borders are in colour and have been formatted. You will therefore create a border and choose colour, thickness, and so on.

FrontPage 2000

To define borders for your table:

1. Select the whole table, right click and select **Table Properties**.
2. Click on the **Style** button. In the dialog box which is displayed, click on **Format, Border** (see Figure 9.13).

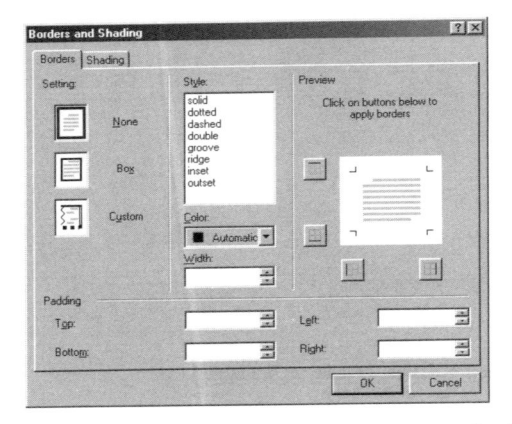

Figure 9.13 Select style, colour and width for your border.

Note that any borders that you might like to select will only affect your table.

3. Choose a yellow double frame. Click several times on **OK** to confirm all the dialog boxes.

To define borders inside cells:

1. Click in the first cell. Right click and select **Cell Properties**.
2. Click on **Style**, then click on **Format, Border**. Apply the same format as for the table. Click on **OK** in each dialog box.
3. Repeat the same procedures for all cells in the table.

Create a second table to insert Van Gogh's paintings (refer to the site). You must create the table as shown in Figure 9.14.

9: Frames, tables and multimedia

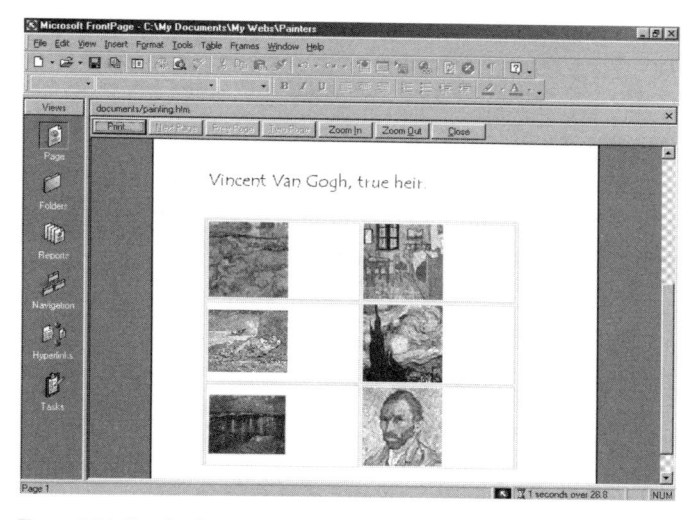

Figure 9.14 Van Gogh pictures.

Modifying tables

You must pre-select all modifications involving a column, a row or a cell before being able to implement changes. You will be able to use the toolbar icons following the same procedures as in Word.

■ Sound

You can insert sound in a Web page. Visitors to your site will then be able to hear music and sound effects.

Inserting sound

You can insert sound in a Web page as a .Wav file or as a MIDI file (bits of music). For this, you must have a sound card and two speakers.

FrontPage 2000

Remember that inserting sound in your site is not compulsory. We will learn here about this option to give you a fuller insight into all the various functions offered by FrontPage.

To insert sound in a Web page:

1. Right click in a page in your site, and select **Page Properties**. Click on the **General** tab (see Figure 9.15).

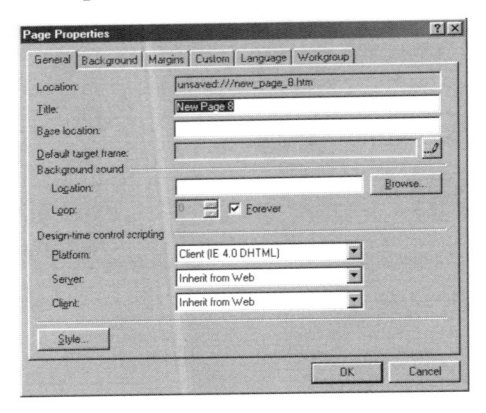

Figure 9.15 You can insert sound in a page in your site.

2. In the **Background sound** box, click in the **Location** option text box. Click on **Browse**.

3. Click on the **Select a file** from your computer icon and select the folder of your choice. Double-click on the file containing the sound to be inserted.

   The path name is displayed in the **Location** box.

4. For the sound file to last throughout the visit of your page, click on the **Forever** option. For the sound file to be repeated a specific number of times, click on the **Loop** option arrow and choose the required number of repetitions. Click on **OK**.

The sound that you have selected is now incorporated into your Web page. Warning: FrontPage does not display any graphical or text symbol to indicate whether you have inserted sound or not.

■ Video clips

Video clips are a way of paying homage to films. We all know the impact of video on our life. FrontPage has the advantage that it allows this incursion into the seventh art, through its video clips. When you insert a video clip, your page will become a much more lively window.

Just like for all good news, we need to dampen our expectations a bit: a video clip lasting a few seconds may require millions of bytes! Your visitors may well get fed up waiting in front of their screen.

Nevertheless, you must be aware that there are several formats of files available for saving a video clip.

- .AVI. Video to Windows. One of the most used formats.
- .GIF(89A). Format for saving animated pictures.
- .MPEG. Multiplatform of video format, the most used format.
- .MOV. QuickTime video format. Created and managed by Apple.

The two most used extensions on the Web are .AVI and .GIF(89A).

Usually, on the Web you will find very short animations (flashing skyscrapers, falling stars, and so on). These types of animation are .GIF files, containing several pictures, hence the term 'animated' GIF.

FrontPage 2000

■ Animated pictures

Retrieve an animated picture you have found on the Web and save it in your picture library. You will then be able to insert it in your FrontPage page.

1. Display the relevant page in **Page** view. Click on **Insert, Picture, Clip Art**.
2. Click on the **Pictures** tab, then click on **Insert**.

   The .GIF file is displayed in your page.

An animated GIF inserted in your FrontPage page is static. It will only become animated when viewed in a browser.

Modifying an animated GIF

FrontPage sees a GIF as a static picture. You can carry out modifications, just as for a static picture.

To modify an animated GIF, follow the same procedures as for modifying pictures shown in previous chapters.

10
Forms and hyperlinks

Forms
Fields
Inserting fields
Data processing
Hyperlinks

FrontPage 2000

In this chapter, you will create a form, you will insert fields in it, learn to process the information sent by the visitors to your site. You will also learn to create some hyperlinks to allow your readers to navigate your site.

■ Forms

Up to now, you have created some Web pages with data. But, on the Web, the notion of interactivity is particularly interesting. It allows you, for example, to retrieve your visitors' opinions. This interactivity is made possible thanks to forms which contain a set of fields which allow you to retrieve the opinions of people who visit your site. To fill in the form, they just need to enter some text, click on some options and check boxes, select choices from a drop-down menu, and so on. A form can include fields, text, tables, pictures, and so on.

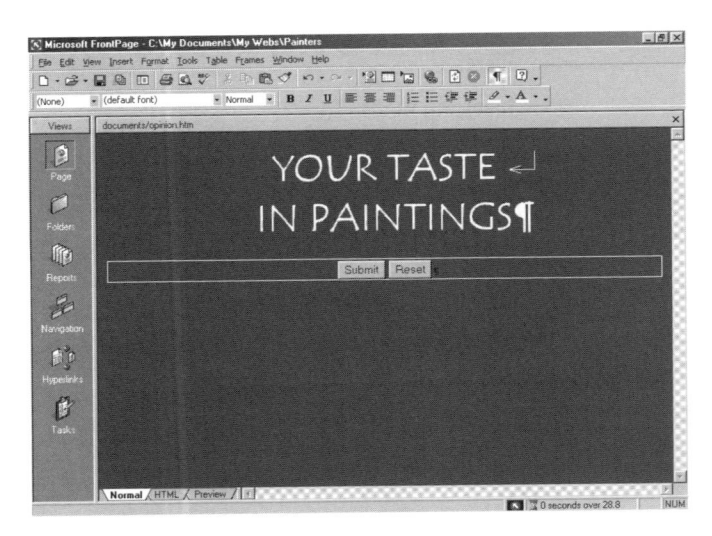

Figure 10.1 You have now inserted a form.

10: Forms and hyperlinks

Creating a form

The first procedure consists in inserting a form in one of your pages. When you create a form, a bar is displayed, with the **Send** and **Reset** buttons. The first allows your visitor to send you the filled form, the second allows you to empty the fields.

To create a form:

1. In the relevant page, click on **Insert, Form**. In our example, open the **Opinion** page in the **Page** view.
2. In the submenu, click on **Form** (see Figure 10.1).

■ Fields

Thanks to the fields, your visitor can supply information or enter data in your form.

Main fields in forms

You will find here a brief description of the various types of fields you can insert in a form:

- **One-Line Text box.** Allows your visitor to enter information directly onto the form (see Figure 10.2).

Figure 10.2 The One-line text box in a Web page.

- **Scrolling Text box.** Allows your visitor to enter text containing several rows (see Figure 10.3).

Figure 10.3 Scrolling text box.

FrontPage 2000

- **Check box.** Allows your visitor to select, or deselect, an option (see Figure 10.4).

Figure 10.4 Check box in a Web page.

- **Radio Button.** Allows your visitor to select a single option (see Figure 10.5).

Figure 10.5 Radio button in a Web page.

- **Drop-Down** menu. Allows your visitor to select a choice from a list (see Figure 10.6).

Figure 10.6 Drop-Down menu in a Web page.

- **Push button.** Allows your visitor to launch any type of action with a simple click on this button (see Figure 10.7).

Figure 10.7 Push button in a Web page.

■ Inserting fields

In the form available in our site, we will always create a page which will tell us the name of our visitors, their address and their e-mail, their preferred art period, their preferred paintings and the page of the site which has been marked.

10: Forms and hyperlinks

Inserting a text box

To insert a text box so that visitors can leave their name, click on **Insert, Form, One-Line Text Box**.

In our site, type Name and Surname and insert a **One-line Text Box** underneath the **Send and Reset** buttons (see Figure 10.8).

Figure 10.8 The view you achieve when you insert a One-line text box.

Defining properties for a text box

For the software to be able to recognise this field's properties, they must be specified.

To define the properties of a text box:

1. Right click in the file, then select **Form Field Properties** (see Figure 10.9).

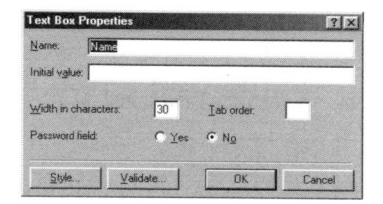

Figure 10.9 This dialog box allows you define the properties of the text box you are inserting.

2. In the **Name** box, type name. Enter 30 in the **Width in characters** option.

The **Initial value** box allows you to specify a default value (irrelevant in this case).

The **Password field** box offers an encrypted entry (irrelevant in this case).

The **Style** button opens a dialog box: it allows you define the style for your field (alignment, frame, font, colour, text).

3. Click on the **Validate** button and you will get the following dialog box (see Figure 10.10).

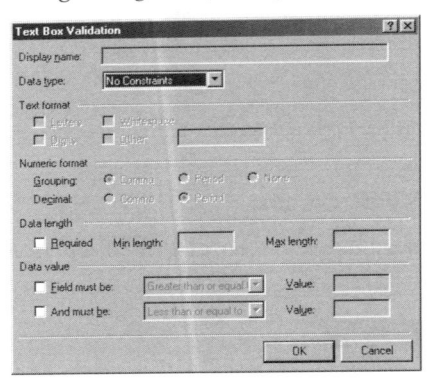

Figure 10.10 In this dialog box, you will set entry constraints and restrictions for the inserted field.

The **Data type** box allows you to select the type of text authorised for this field (see Table 10.1).

4. Click on the **Data type** arrow and select **Text**. In the **Text format** box, select the **Letters** option. Click on **OK** in the **Confirm** dialog box of the text box, then click on **OK** in the **Properties** dialog box of the **simple text** box.

10: Forms and hyperlinks

The following table lists the various choices available in the Data Type box.

Type	Format
Text	Lets you enter any character
All	Lets you enter figures. You can authorise or forbid entry of commas and/or full stops.
Numbers	Lets you enter figures. You can authorise commas or full stops for decimal points.

Table 10.1 The various types of data in a field.

Inserting a Scrolling Text Box

Still in the same page, we will insert a box where visitors will be able to specify their postal address and their e-mail address.

To insert a drop-down text box, place the cursor where you wish this to be. Click on **Insert, Form, Scrolling Text Box**.

For our site, type **Address**, then insert a scrolling text box underneath the one-line text box. Then, define the properties of the **Scrolling Text Box** as demonstrated previously, but without selecting any constraints.

Inserting an option check box field

The check boxes let your visitors define a choice from a list.

To insert a check box field, click on **Insert, Form, Check box**.

FrontPage 2000

After entering their name, surname and address, visitors will start expressing their opinions on your site. Let's create a field where they can select the impressionist painter they prefer.

For our site, type **Preferred painter**, then insert seven check boxes underneath the drop-down text box. Enter the name of each painter against each check box.

Defining Properties check box

For FrontPage to be able to manage answers to a question, you must instruct the software that the various possible answers form a group of options.

To do this:

1. Point to the first check box, right click and select **Form Field Properties** (see Figure 10.11).

Figure 10.11 In this dialog box you must define the Check Box Properties.

2. To name the group of options, type Painters in the **Name** box.
3. Select the **Not checked** option in the **Initial state** box.

    This box allows you to specify the default check box. In our example, no check box is active by default.
4. Click on **OK**. Repeat procedures 1 to 4 for each check box.

10: Forms and hyperlinks

Inserting multiple-choice check boxes

Multiple-choice check boxes allow visitors to select several choices from a suggestion list.

To insert a multiple-choice check boxes field, click on **Insert, Form, Radio Button**.

> *The multiple-choice check boxes properties are defined according to the same rules as the option check boxes.*

Inserting a drop-down menu field

A drop-down menu allows you to create a list from which visitors can select a choice.

To insert a drop-down menu, click on **Insert, Form, Drop-Down Menu**.

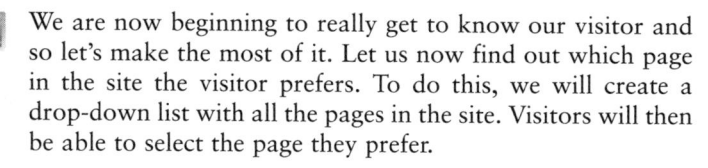

We are now beginning to really get to know our visitor and so let's make the most of it. Let us now find out which page in the site the visitor prefers. To do this, we will create a drop-down list with all the pages in the site. Visitors will then be able to select the page they prefer.

For our site, type **Preferred Pages**, then insert a drop-down menu underneath the box containing the option check boxes.

Defining Properties for a drop-down menu field

You must define the properties for this field so that it is displayed in an appropriate size in the page.

To define the properties of the drop-down menu field:

1. In the field, right click, then select **Form Field Properties** (see Figure 10.12).

FrontPage 2000

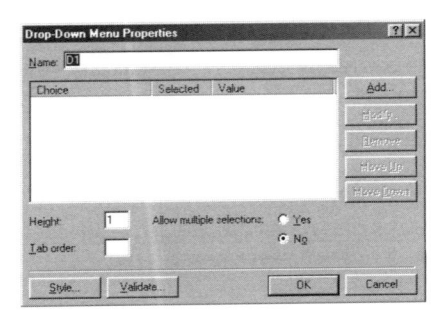

Figure 10.12 You must specify all the drop-down menu properties in this dialog box.

2. Enter **pages** to name the drop-down menu, then click on the **Add** button. In the **Add Choice** dialog box which is displayed, you must enter the first item in the list. For our site, type Index in the **Choice** box, then click on **OK**.

3. Again in the drop-down menu properties dialog box, click **new** in the **Add** button, then type the name of another page and click on **OK**. Repeat the same procedures for all the pages in the site.

4. When you have entered all the pages, click on **OK** in the **Drop-Down Menu Properties** dialog box.

*If you are not satisfied with the page order, in the drop-down menu click the name of the page you wish to shift in the form field Properties dialog box. Click on **Move up** or on **Move down**.*

Defining the Properties of Command buttons

Your form is finished. You have inserted all the fields required for visitors to be able to give you their impressions concerning your site. The information will be sent with the form buttons that you have created at the beginning of the chapter. However, if you wish to insert a customised command button, you must define its properties.

10: Forms and hyperlinks

To define the properties for a command button:

1. Right click on the command button, then select **Form Field Properties** and you will get the following (see Figure 10.13).

Figure 10.13 You must define properties for command buttons.

2. In the **Name** box, type the required name. In the **Value/label** box, type the wording that you want to see on your button. Check the option to be activated in the **Button type**. Click on **OK**.

This is the form that you must create by the end of this chapter (see Figure 10.14).

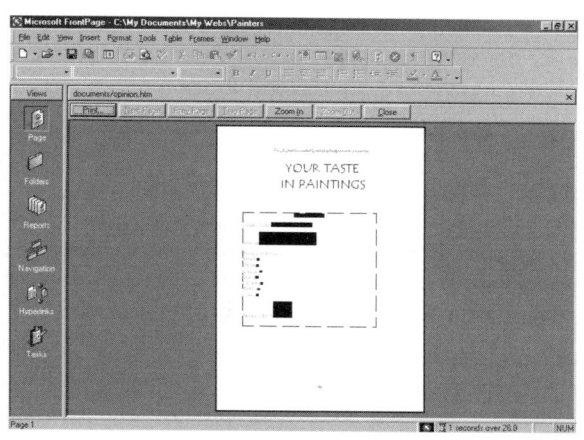

Figure 10.14 You have now inserted a form.

■ Data processing

We have placed all the form fields on our page and set the properties for each field. Your visitors will visit your site, fill the various fields and send their replies. To be able to receive them, you must process them and save them to a file.

To process data from a form, you must define properties:

1. Right click in the form page, then select **Form Properties**.
   - The **Send to** option is ticked as the default.
   - In the **File name** box, a file name is already suggested. Do not change it – it is perfect for our purposes.
   - You can complete the **E-Mail Address** box. You will also receive result forms as e-mail messages.
2. Fill in the **Form name** box, then click on **OK**.

■ Hyperlinks

A hyperlink on a Web page links to a page somewhere else on the same site or even to another site. The final destination of the hyperlink can often be a page within the site – however, it could also link straight to a picture, an address, a multimedia file, and so on.

Hyperlinks are embedded in the text or in the picture on a page. They provide textual or graphic indices for their destination. In the site that we are creating, for example, the word History indicates that the hyperlink takes you to a page describing the history of the Impressionists.

In the browser, the hyperlinks are underlined and are displayed in a specific colour. In a picture, the hyperlinks are invisible; the pointer, which takes the shape of a hand when you hover over a hyperlink, is your only guide.

10: Forms and hyperlinks

By clicking on a hyperlink, browsers access and display the page. The hyperlink is in URL code (*Uniform Resource Locator*).

Creating hyperlinks to take you to other pages

You can create your own hyperlinks between pages within the same site.

You will create a hyperlink between the word **History** on the Homepage and the **History** page.

1. Select the word which should be the hyperlink. Select **History** in the **Index** page.
2. Click on the **Hyperlink** icon in the Standard toolbar (see Figure 10.15). Double-click on the **Paintings** page in the list. You can also click on the required page, then on **OK**.

   In the site, the word **History** appears underlined, which indicates that it is now a hyperlink.

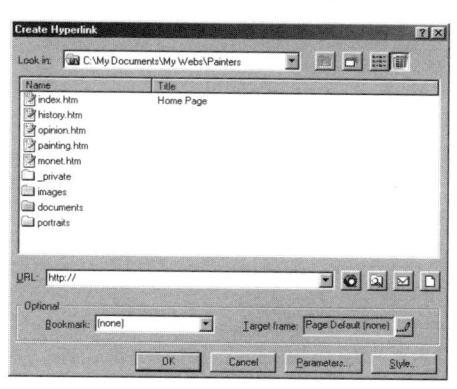

Figure 10.15 Specifying the destination page for the selected word.

Using the hyperlink icon, link the words 'Their best works of art' to the 'Paintings' page, 'The father of' to the Monet page, and 'Your preferences' to the 'Opinions' page.

Creating a picture which interacts with another page

You can create pictures which take you to another page in the site. The procedure is the same as for creating a hyperlink.

It is imperative that each page should allow you to return to the Homepage. To do this, copy then paste the rose on each page in the site. Reduce it to a 50 pixels size, then deactivate its position (see previous chapters).

You will now create a link between the rose placed in the **History** page and the **Index** page.

To create an interactive picture between two pages of a site:

1. Select the **rose**.
2. Click on the **Hyperlink** icon in the Standard toolbar. Double click on the **Index** page.

Creating a hyperlink in the same page

A hyperlink which refers to a place in the same page is known as a bookmark.

To create a bookmark:

1. Select the first word. Click on **Insert, Bookmark** (see Figure 10.16).

Figure 10.16 Creating the first bookmark in the Bookmark dialog box.

10: Forms and hyperlinks

2. Click on **OK**. Again in the page, select the word to which the link refers. Click on the **Hyperlink** icon. In the dialog box, click on the Bookmark drop-down list arrow and select the first bookmark that you have created. Click on **OK** to confirm.

*To delete a bookmark, click on **Insert**, **Bookmark**. In the list, select the bookmark to be deleted, then click on the **Clear** button. Click on **OK** to confirm.*

Creating hyperlinks to another site

While surfing the Web, we have discovered a site which has all the paintings by the greatest painters. We have taken down its address and we are going to create a hyperlink between our site and this 'museum' site

To create a hyperlink to another site:

1. Select the word you wish to use as a hyperlink. In our site, select '**A walk through the museum**' in the **Index** page.
2. Click on the **Hyperlink** icon in the Standard toolbar. In the dialog box, type the site address in the URL box. For our site, type **http://metalab.unc.edu/wm/paint/auth**. Then click on **OK**.

Deleting a hyperlink

You may find that you no longer want a link.

To delete a hyperlink, select the hyperlinked word. Right click and select **Hyperlink Properties**. Press on the **Del** key, then click on **OK**.

We will see in the next chapter how to test the hyperlinks and modify their colour.

Site management

Managing hyperlinks
Organising pages and pictures
Site structure
Work organisation

FrontPage 2000

In this chapter, you will learn to organise your site, pictures, pages and structure navigation. You will also see how to create a site summary, create reports on its contents, and so on.

■ Managing hyperlinks

We have previously learnt how to create hyperlinks. Let us now see how to manage these links.

Defining links colour

FrontPage lets you assign a colour for your hyperlinks. This is important for managing links, whether they are visited or not, and to signal the active link.

Of course, this concerns visits to your page by a surfer.

To manage links colour:

1. In the relevant page, right click and select **Page Properties**.
2. Click on the **Background** tab (see Figure 11.1).

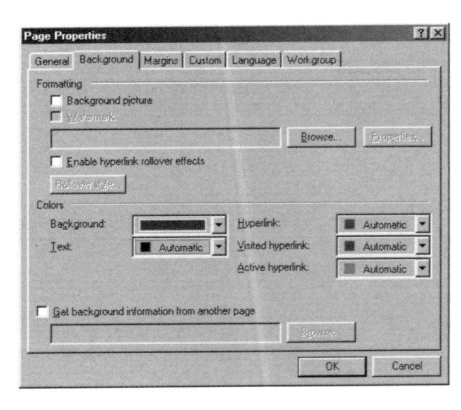

Figure 11.1 This tab allows you to modify the colour of your links.

11: Site management

3. Click on the **Hyperlink** option arrow, then on the colour you want activated. Click on the **Visited Hyperlink** option arrow, then click on the colour you want activated. In the box for our Web site, apply yellow to all the hyperlinks, white to all visited links and black to all active links. Click on **OK**.

4. Repeat this procedure for each page in our Web site.

Checking links

Good Website management involves checking hyperlinks. In practice, if the links do not work or are incorrect, visitors will be unable to navigate the site and will just go away.

To verify hyperlinks:

1. After opening the site, click on the **Reports** view in the **Views** bar to display the reporting toolbar (see Figure 11.2).

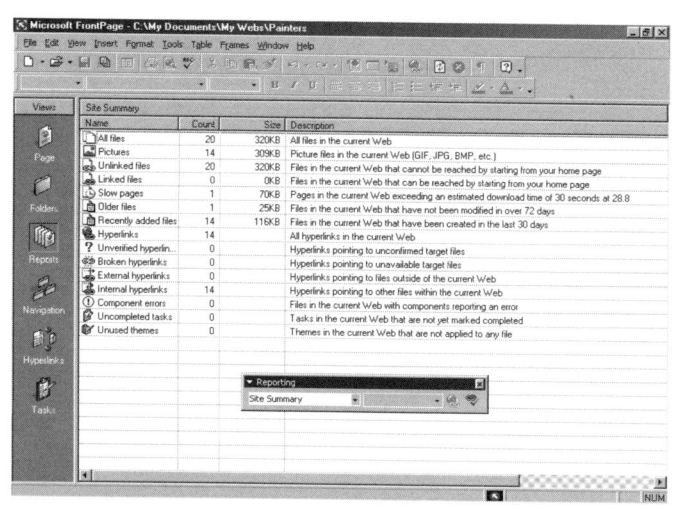

Figure 11.2 The Reports view allows you to check whether your links work.

FrontPage 2000

2. Click on the **Verify Hyperlinks** icon in the **Reporting** toolbar (see Figure 11.3).

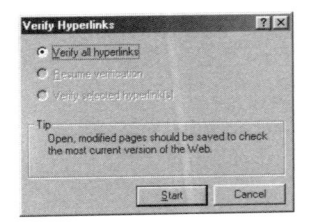

Figure 11.3 Starting the hyperlinks verification procedure.

Click on the required option. For our site, select **Verify all Hyperlinks**, then click on **Start** (see Figure 11.4).

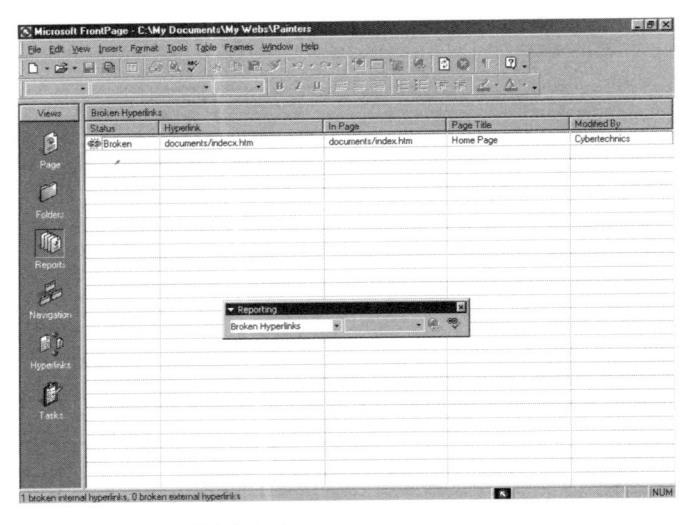

Figure 11.4 A hyperlink is broken.

11: Site management

Repairing broken links

If one or more hyperlinks are broken, you must repair them. A broken hyperlink takes you to an incorrect URL destination and displays an error message when visitors click on it.

To repair a broken hyperlink:

1. You must first display the broken hyperlink. To do this, click on **View, Reports, Broken Hyperlink**.

2. Right click on the broken hyperlink, then click on **Edit Page**. The page is displayed. Once you have selected the hyperlink, click on the **Hyperlink** icon. Specify the correct URL. For our site, delete the old URL and replace it with www.marmottan.fr. Click on **Browse** to look for the page or the file.

3. To repair all the link occurrences on all pages in the site, click on **Change in all pages**. To repair some links only, click on **Change in selected pages**, then select the relevant pages. Click on **Replace hyperlink with**. You can also right click on the hyperlink, in the Reports view, then select **Edit Hyperlink** (see Figure 11.5). Enter the new address and click on **OK** to confirm (see Figure 11.6).

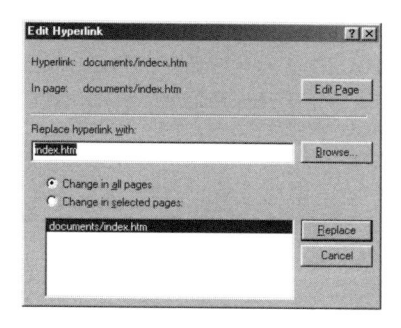

Figure 11.5 Modify the link address in the Edit hyperlink dialog box.

FrontPage 2000

Broken Hyperlinks				
Status	Hyperlink	In Page	Page Title	Modified By
? Edited	documents/indecx.htm	documents/index.htm	Home Page	Cybertechnics

Figure 11.6 In the Reports view, the Edit option is displayed in the previously incorrect link.

Viewing all hyperlinks

In the Hyperlinks view you can view all the links that you have created graphically, which is quite an attractive idea!

To view all the hyperlinks in a site, click on the **Hyperlinks** view in the **Views** bar. In the **Folder List,** click on the page whose hyperlinks you wish to display. In the area to the right, the hyperlinks are displayed, together with the destination item.

Testing in the browser

Come on, have some fun: view your pages in the browser. You will now be able to enjoy the fruits of your hard labour, directly on site.

To view your pages in the browser:

1. Open the site, then display the site start page in **Page** view. Click on **File, Preview in Browser** (see Figure 11.7).

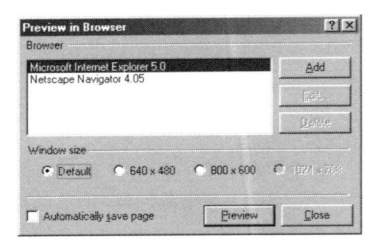

Figure 11.7 Specify how you wish your site to be displayed when you preview it in the browser.

174

2. Click on **Preview**. The site start page is displayed in the browser. Click on the various hyperlinks to view the other pages. Click on **File, Close** to leave the browser.

■ Organising pages and pictures

If you have followed us faithfully chapter by chapter, you are now the proud owner of a site on Impressionist paintings made up of several pages which are as beautiful as they are interesting. Now you need to learn how to organise the structure and the navigation for your site. Let us first look at the organisation of your pages and pictures.

Importing pages

In our example, we have created the pages directly in the site. However, FrontPage allows you to use existing pages, stored somewhere else on your hard disk.

To import existing pages:

1. Click on **File, Import** (see Figure 11.8).

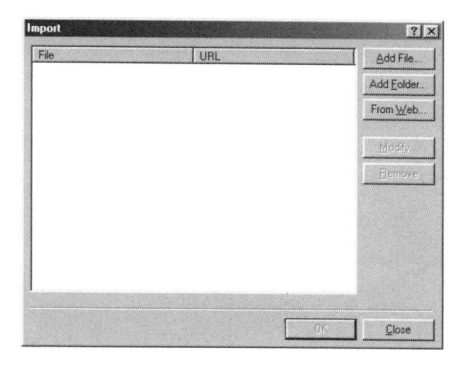

Figure 11.8 Importing pages stored on your hard disk.

FrontPage 2000

2. Click on **Add File**. Select the required page, then double-click on it. This will be displayed in the **Import** dialog box list. Repeat the same procedures until you have selected all the pages to be imported. Click on **Close**. Now you simply need to simply create and organise the site with the pages that you have just imported.

Organising pictures

We know that you have placed your pages in a folder created in previous chapters, so all your pictures are stored in this folder. It is however better for these to be stored in the Picture folders.

To classify your pictures:

1. In the Folders view, double click on the **Documents** folder (see Figure 11.9).

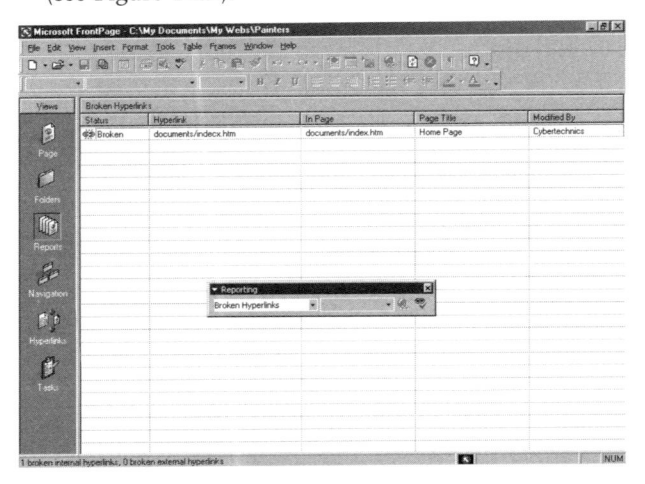

Figure 11.9 The pictures are stored in the created folder.

2. Select all the pictures, apart from those called **Portrait**. Click in the selection, then drag it into the **Picture** folders (see Figure 11.10).

176

11: Site management

Figure 11.10 FrontPage renames pictures when you move them.

3. Select all pictures called **Portrait**. Click and drag them into the **Portraits** folder.

*When renaming pages, FrontPage offers to upgrade hyperlinks according to the changes made. Confirm by clicking **OK**.*

Site summary

You can ask FrontPage to audit your site. You will then know exactly what your site contains.

To count the pictures in a site, click on **View, Reports, Site Summary** (see Figure 11.11).

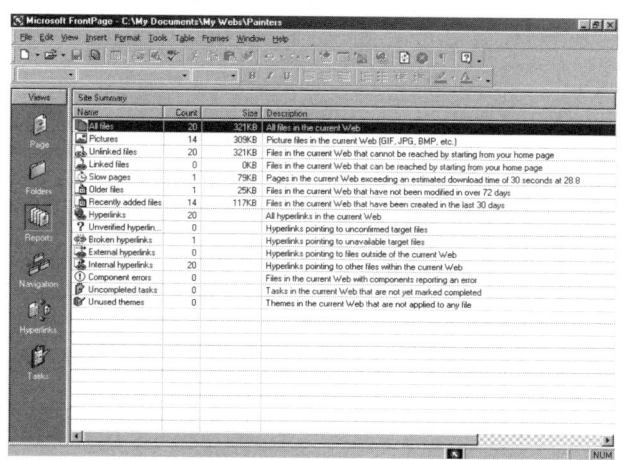

Figure 11.11 FrontPage displays a comprehensive site summary.

FrontPage 2000

Identifying slow-loading pages

You can ask FrontPage to check if there are pages in your site which are very slow to download from the Web. This is quite useful because, in this way, you can assess approximately how long it would take for each page to download from the Web, and possibly modify the slow ones so that they can take less time to download.

To identify the slow-loading pages in your site, click on **View, Reports, Site Summary**. In the site summary, double-click on the entry Pages in the current Web exceeding an estimated download time of 30 seconds at 28.8. A new table is displayed which lists all the slow pages and their estimated downloading time (see Figure 11.12).

Slow Pages						
Name	Title	Download Time	Size	Type	In Folder	Modified Date
history.htm	documents/history.htm	41 Seconds	4KB	htm	documents	09/08/99 10:34 AM

Figure 11.12 You can identify pages which download slowly and modify them if necessary.

Sorting files

To organise the pages in your site more effectively, you can sort them by date.

- To display the files which have been recently added to your site, click on **View, Reports, Recently Added Files**.
- To display the files which have been recently modified in your site, click on **View, Reports, Recently Changed Files**.
- To display old files in your site, click on **View, Reports, Older Files**.
- To display non linked files, click on **View, Reports, Unlinked Files**.

11: Site management

■ Site structure

The structure of a site is in actual fact its navigation mode. In practice, this is what dictates the organisation of your pages, where to insert navigation bars, and so on. The navigation structure determines the order of pages and the way visitors will 'walk through' your site.

Defining the structure

You will define the position for your pages in the Impressionists site.

To organise the structure of a site:

1. Open the site. In our example, open the **Painters** site. Click on the **Navigation** view. Close all the folders, apart from the Documents folder which contains the pages for your site (see Figure 11.13).

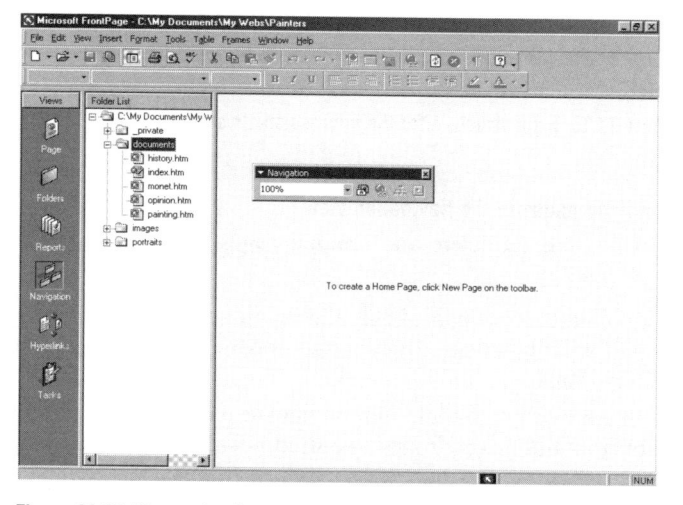

Figure 11.13 The navigation structure only contains the current start page.

FrontPage 2000

2. In the Folder List, click on the **History** page. Without releasing the button, drag it under the start page, in the area to the right (see Figure 11.14). Do the same thing for each page in your site in order to achieve what is shown in Figure 11.15.

Figure 11.14 Insert the History page underneath the home page.

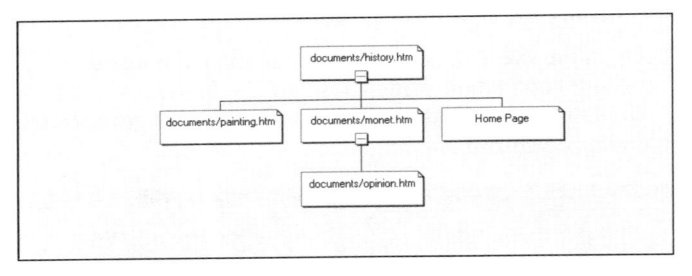

Figure 11.15 Final structure for the Impressionists site.

Managing pages in the Navigation view

You can create, delete and rename pages in the Navigation view.

- To create a new page, bring the pointer into the box where you wish to create a new page and right click. Click on **New Page**.
- To move a page, click on the relevant page, hold down the button and drag it to the required position.
- To delete a page, click on it and press on the **Del** key.

11: Site management

Printing the site structure

As you create your site, its structure evolves. It may be useful to print it out.

To print the structure of a site, in the Navigation view click on the **Print** icon in the Standard toolbar.

Modifying your site

The Web is never static, and neither is your site. You can therefore modify, enhance, delete pages from your site, even when it is published on a server. Carry out your modifications as shown in previous chapters, then publish the update (if you want to know more about publishing procedures, refer to Chapter 12).

■ Work organisation

In our example, we have made the assumption that you have been working on the site by yourself. This will be true if you use FrontPage for personal purposes. On the other hand, if you must create a site for professional purposes and there are a number of different people working on the same project, you will definitely need to organise the work by assigning specific tasks to each author. To do this, FrontPage offers the Tasks view, which lists the tasks required for creating the site. A task is a specific type of job to be carried out, within the framework of the site construction (retrieving pictures, recording sound, and so on). Therefore, this part is really aimed at people working within companies.

This mode displays, in columns, the status (in progress, completed, and so on), the task name, the name of the person assigned to the task, the relevant page for the task, the task modification and a brief task description.

FrontPage 2000

- To display the **Tasks** view, click on the **Tasks** icon in the Views bar.
- To create a task:

1. In the **Tasks** view, click on **Edit, Task, Add Task** (see Figure 11.16).

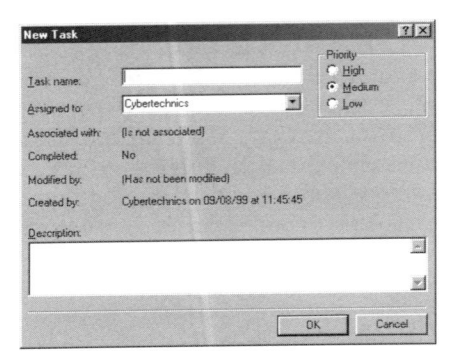

Figure 11.16 In this dialog box, you will create a task for your site.

2. In the **Task name** box, assign a name to the task. In the **Assigned to** box, type the name of the person who is responsible for the task. In the **Priority** box, click on the option you wish to activate (high, medium or low).

3. In the **Description** box, type your task name. Click on **OK**.

   The task that you have just created is displayed in the area of the **Tasks** view.

11: Site management

- To delete a task, click on the relevant task, then press the **Del** key. In the dialog box which is displayed, click **Yes** to confirm that you really want to delete it.
- To modify a task:

1. Right click on the task to be modified. Select **Edit task**.
2. Carry out the required modifications. Click on **OK**.

When an assigned task is completed, you must record this.

To mark a task as completed, right click on the relevant task, then click on **Mark as Completed**.

12
Publishing and security

- IP
- Connections
- Publishing your site
- Servers
- Configuring the Administrator
- Server properties
- Securing your server
- Testing the Web server
- Visiting your site

FrontPage 2000

In this chapter, we will learn the procedures for Intranet publishing and for securing your site. Your computer will act as a server and you will find out how to choose a server from the two suggested by FrontPage. You will also learn how to secure your site.

■ IP

Unfortunately, when we come to servers, we are not all equal. In practice, some users may have their own server (those who work for a company which has direct Internet access), others, and this is the vast majority, do not have a personal server. These users must therefore 'rent' space on an IP (Internet Provider) server.

When you create a site and wish to post it on the Web, you have to comply with a certain number of conditions to make accessing your site both easy and practical. These conditions are difficult to describe in detail. In practice, you will need to have an installation device which will allow, for example, several people to access it at the same time. Just imagine: for ten people who call up your server, you need ten entry lines! For your site to be available anywhere in the world and at any time, your computer must be permanently on, seven days a week, twenty-four hours a day.

Space allocation with an IP allows you to guarantee the required conditions for publishing a site:

- easy access;
- quick Internet connection;
- permanent site access.

12: Publishing and security

An IP fulfils all these conditions. Through your IP server, visitors to your site will be able to view your Web pages.

> *Before renting commercial space with an IP to publish your Web site, make sure that your IP caters for FrontPage extensions. If this is not the case, publishing procedures will be different.*

Companies which have local networks have a Web-ready server, therefore they will not need an IP.

When you publish a site on an IP server, remember that all files which make up your site will be copied from your computer to the server, but the original will still be on your computer! When you create a site and you publish it with an IP, also bear in mind that usually the price you are going to be charged for space is related to the space used. The more files your site has, the more you will need to pay for your space.

■ Connections

If you rent space with an Internet provider, you will publish your site through a TCP/IP connection.

This connection is via a modem that you will have installed on your computer.

If you have not yet implemented the various Internet connections, carry out the following procedures so that your connections can be implemented.

There are various connections:

- TCP/IP protocol;
- Remote Access to the Windows 95 or 98 network;
- IP connection.

FrontPage 2000

To install a TCP/IP protocol:

1. On the Desktop, click on **Start, Settings, Control Panel**. Double-click on the **Network** icon (see Figure 12.1).

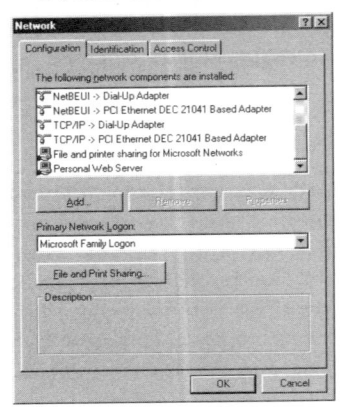

Figure 12.1 The Network dialog box lets you add the TCP/IP protocol.

2. Click on the **Add** button, then click on the **Dial-Up** icon.
3. Click on **Add**, then on **detected net drivers**. Click on **OK**.
4. In **The following network components are installed** dialog box, click on **TCP/IP**, then on **Properties**.
5. Click on the IP Address tab, then check **Obtain an IP address automatically**. Click on the **WINS Configuration** tab, then check **Disable WINS resolution**.
6. Click on the **Gateway** tab, then type the number provided by your IP. Click on the **DNS Configuration** tab, then check **Enable DNS**. Type your IP name in the **Host** box.
7. In the **Domain** box, type your IP domain. In the **DNS Server Search Order** box, type the primary DNS supplied by your IP, then click on **Add**. In the **DNS Server Search Order** box, type the secondary DNS supplied by your IP, then click on **Add**.

12: Publishing and security

8. Click on **OK** in the **TCP/IP Properties** dialog box. Click on **OK** in the **Network** dialog box, then click on **Yes** in the dialog box which is displayed.

To install Windows 98 Remote Network access:

1. On the Desktop, click on **Start, Settings, Control Panel**.
2. Double-click on **Add/Remove programs**. Click on the **Windows Setup** tab, on the **Communications** icon, then on the **Details** button.
3. Tick the **Dial-Up Networking** check box. Click on **OK** in the **Communications** dialog box, then click on **OK** in the **Add/Remove programs** dialog box.

To create your IP connection:

1. On the Windows Desktop, click on **Start, Programs, Accessories, Communications, Dial-Up Networking** (see Figure 12.2).

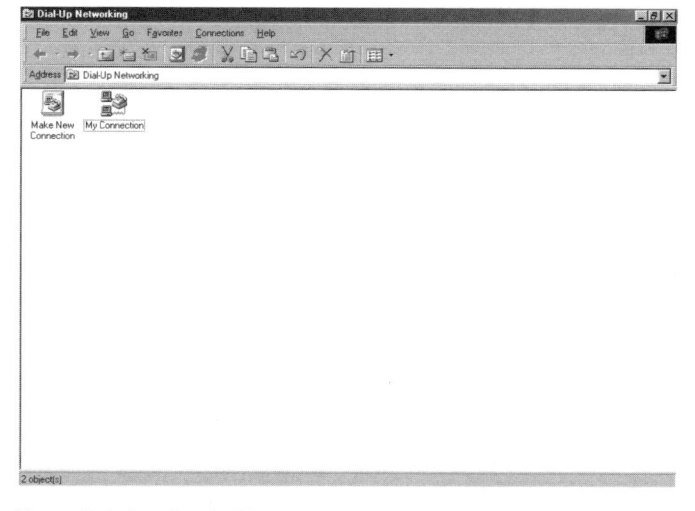

Figure 12.2 Creating the IP connection.

2. Double-click on **Make New Connection**. Enter your IP name in the **Type a name for the computer you are dialling** box. Click on the **Select a device** box arrow. Select your modem from the list.

3. Click on **Next**. Enter the various numbers in the relevant boxes.

4. Click on **Next**, then on **Finish**.

■ Publishing your site

Once the connection has been implemented and tested, you will be able to publish your site on the IP server. The following publishing procedures are for readers whose IP caters for FrontPage extensions.

To publish your FrontPage Web site, which means sending it to your IP server, you must follow a specific procedure that FrontPage has decided to make as simple as possible.

Publishing with FrontPage extensions

Publishing in this case is carried out from the Folders view.

1. Open the site, then click on **Publish Web**. You can also click on **File, Web**.

   The **Publish Web** dialog box is displayed (see Figure 12.3).

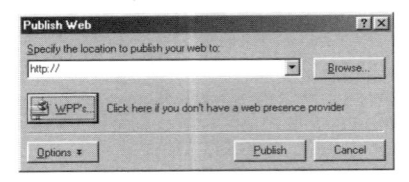

Figure 12.3 This dialog box lets you specify the required server.

12: Publishing and security

2. Click on the text box arrow.

   The generic name of your IP server is displayed.

3. Click on it.

   You must assign a name to your site.

4. Click in the text box, delete the current site name, then type the new name. Click on **OK**.

   FrontPage sends the set of files which make up your site to your Internet provider.

   You can follow the transmission protocol in the status bar which displays its progress.

   When the transmission process is completed, a dialog box is displayed.

Your IP only has a copy of your site. The original is still in FrontPage.

Publishing without FrontPage extensions

We mentioned earlier that your IP may not cater for FrontPage extensions. If this is the case, the publishing procedure is different. You must use file transfer software (FTP). The FTP used in the following procedure is compatible with Windows 95, 98 or Windows NT It is called ftp32.zip. You must download this software.

To download the file transfer software, launch your browser. In the Address box, type **ftp://ftp.sct.fr/pub/pc/windows98/ftp/ws ftp32.zip**. The browser will download the software. This program is compressed, you must decompress it to be able to use it.

To download the decompression software, launch your browser. In the Address box, type **ftp://ftp.sct.fr/pub/pc/windows98/compression/winzip95.exe**. The browser will download the software.

FrontPage 2000

This is shareware software, which means that it is freely available for use within a time limit. If you wish to carry on using it, you must pay a fee to the authors.

When you have decompressed the transfer software, you will be able to use it to publish your FrontPage Web site. The first procedure, before publishing your site, is to launch the transfer software as follows:

1. Start Windows Explorer. Click on the folder containing the software. Double-click on **WS_FTP32**.

2. Click on **Cancel**. In the top left window, double click on the two dots.

3. Click on the scroll arrow to find the folder containing the site. Double-click on the folder.

   The bottom window displays the list of files in your site.

4. Click on **Connect**. In the **Host Name** box, type the domain name supplied by your IP. In the **User Id** box, type your connection log-in (supplied by your IP). In the **Password** box, type your password (supplied by your IP). In the **Remote Host** box, type the path for the space allocated by your IP. Click on **OK**.

5. The **Connecting to the Internet** dialog box is displayed. Click on **Connect**.

   Your site transfer is now executed: your site is published on the Web.

■ Servers

The Intranet concept concerns companies working with a local network. You will configure your computer as a server. You can also publish your site on your company's Intranet.

12: Publishing and security

FrontPage offers two types of servers:

- FrontPage personal Web server;
- Microsoft personal Web server.

You can use either of these two servers. In our case, we prefer to use Microsoft personal Web server. And we are going to explain why.

FrontPage personal Web server

This software comes with the basic FrontPage product family. It works very well for testing pages created on your site, but is not very impressive in terms of capacity and it is very poor as far as security is concerned.

Microsoft personal Web server

This software comes with FrontPage 2000 premium pack. As opposed to FrontPage personal Web server, it fulfils most of the conditions for very satisfying usage. This high-performance software allows you to secure your server quite satisfactorily. Only one black mark: it does not work under Windows NT. If you work in this environment, talk to the IT manager in your company who will be able to advise you as to what to do.

Installing and uninstalling a server

The installation and uninstalling of the Microsoft server is carried out in Administrator.

Administrator is the tool which allows you to manage the installation ports. In practice, when you install software such as a server, you must specify the connection port. Let us use an example. Your computer has a number of peripherals such as a printer, a modem, an external CD, and so on, whose input and output is through a 'port'. It is the same with servers: they

FrontPage 2000

are connected through a specific port. Administrator manages these 'ports'. In the case of an e-mail server, the port is 110. In the case of a Web server, the port is 80.

If two servers are connected through the same port, there will be a bottleneck and nothing will work. You will therefore instruct Administrator that the current port 80 connection is no longer valid.

To uninstall the FrontPage personal Web server:

1. Start Windows Explorer.
2. Double-click on the **Program Files** folder.
3. Click on the **Microsoft FrontPage** folder.
4. Double-click on **FrontPage Server Administrator**.

   The FrontPage server Administrator window is displayed. The top left list shows the used port number (80).

5. Click on 80 to display the information regarding the server at this address (FrontPage personal Web server). Click on **Uninstall**, then on **OK**.

When you have uninstalled the FrontPage personal Web server and freed port 80 in Administrator, you can install the Microsoft personal Web server:

1. Insert the Office CD-ROM in your drive. Launch the installation program.
2. Click on **Customize**. Follow the standard procedures to install the Microsoft server.

   Usually the computer will prompt you to restart it.

When the Microsoft personal Web server is installed, an icon is displayed in the task bar. This means that the server is active. If this icon is not displayed, you must activate it manually for the chosen server to become active.

1. Click on **Start, Settings, Control Panel** (see Figure 12.4).

12: Publishing and security

Figure 12.4 The personal Web server icon is displayed in the Control Panel.

2. Double-click on the personal Web server icon. Click on the **Startup** tab (see Figure 12.5).

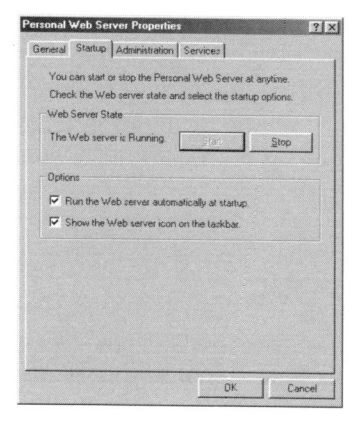

Figure 12.5 The Personal Web Server Properties dialog box is displayed.

FrontPage 2000

3. Click on **Start** in the Web server status box. Click on **OK**.

Now that the Microsoft personal Web server is launched, you must signal its presence to the server Administrator.

To inform the Administrator of the new server:

1. Start Windows Explorer. Double-click on the **Program Files** folder.
2. Click on the **Microsoft FrontPage** folder. Double-click on **FrontPage Server Administrator**.

   The FrontPage Server Administrator window is displayed.
3. Click on **Install**, then click on the **Type of server** option arrow. Select **Microsoft Personal Web Server**. Click on **OK**.

   The Administrator displays a confirm dialog box.
4. Click on **OK**.

   The Administrator prompts you to create a summary of the modification pages or of the changes to the server (this concerns the security of your site, which we will introduce at the end of this chapter).
5. Click on **OK**.

   The Administrator restarts the server so that the modifications becomes effective. The new configuration is displayed.

The server is installed on your machine and everybody in your company can now visit your site by connecting to your computer.

■ Configuring the Administrator

As we have seen before, Administrator is where you choose your server and you manage its port. Administrator allows you other interesting configurations.

12: Publishing and security

To configure Administrator:

1. Start Windows Explorer. Double-click on the **Program Files** folder. Click on the **Microsoft FrontPage** folder. Double click on **FrontPage Server Administrator**.

   Check that **Create Web pages** is activated. This function allows you to modify a Web page directly on the server while it is active. When this option is deactivated, pages cannot be modified. This is write-protection (as for a floppy disk).

2. Click on **Authoring**, then on your choice. Click on **OK**.

   You will define the administrators, that is, the users who have access to your Web server sites. These administrators may read, modify, add or delete Web pages. They can also define who will be allowed to get into the site to modify it, and so on.

3. Click on **Security**. In the **Name** box, type the administrators of your choice.

4. In the **Web site Name** box, leave `<Web Site root>` active if you want these people to be granted access to all sites on your server. Otherwise, type the name of the relevant site.

   A confirmation dialog box is displayed.

5. Click on **OK**, then click on **OK** in the **Server Administrator** dialog box. Click on **Close** in Administrator.

■ Server Properties

A server is not a simple unit, it has a number of properties that you must configure. These properties concern the creation of Web pages, start page, start up, automatic server execution, and so on. You will define these various options in the personal Web server properties dialog box.

FrontPage 2000

To display the personal Web server properties dialog box, right click on the personal Web server icon in the task bar of the Windows Desktop (on the right, next to the clock), then click on **Properties** to obtain the following: (see Figure 12.6).

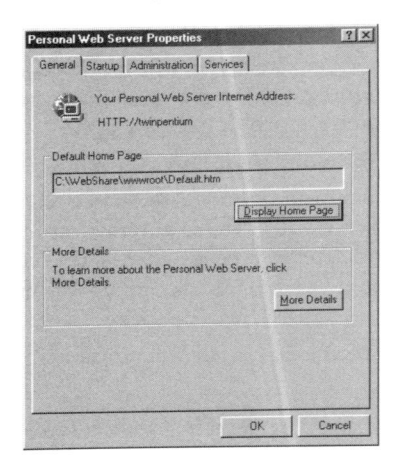

Figure 12.6 The General tab in the Server Properties dialog box.

The General tab of the Server Properties dialog box

Your server's URL is displayed, usually **http://** followed by your computer name; your start page path is displayed underneath.

From this tab, you can view your site's home page by clicking on **Display Home Page**, then display the help sections of the personal Web server by clicking on **More details**.

The Startup tab of the Server Properties dialog box

You can open or close the Web server by clicking on **start** or **stop** in the Web server status box. You can also choose automatic startup and show the Web server icon on the task bar (which is active by default) by ticking the **Run the Web server automatically at startup** and **Show Web server** icon on the task bar.

12: Publishing and security

The Administration tab of the Server Properties dialog box

This tab is in fact a Web-based application which allows you to manage the server in a browser. Click on the **Administration** button (see Figure 12.7).

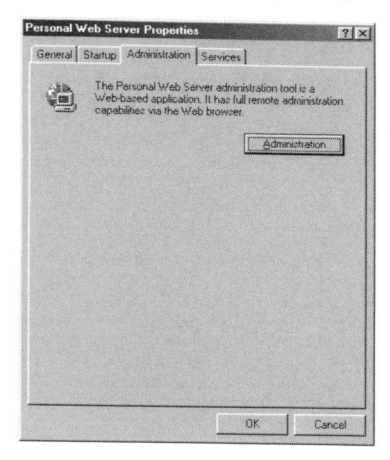

Figure 12.7 The Web server administration tool.

All these configurations are under-used. You should however remember that you can use them to define the users who are granted access to your Web pages.

> *Before being able to use the administration application, your Web server should not be used as a file or a printer server.*

The Services tab of the Server Properties dialog box

This tab allows you to define the Internet services which are available from your server.

The personal Web server looks after two types of services:

- **HTTP (HyperText Transport Protocol)**. Lets you access Web pages on the Internet or Intranet.

FrontPage 2000

- **FTP** (File Transfer Protocol). Allows you to download files from your computer or in the FTP directory.

The **Services** box allows you to modify the properties of a service: click on it, then click on **Properties** (see Figure 12.8).

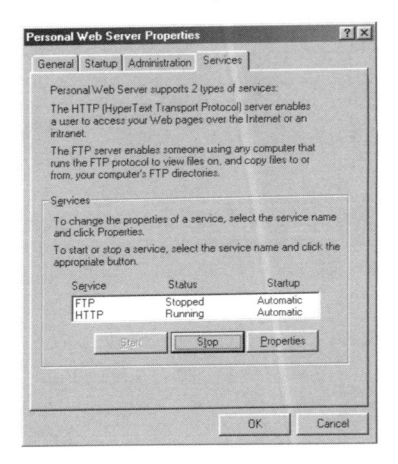

Figure 12.8 The Services box lets you change the properties of a service.

In this dialog box, you can modify the properties of a service. In the HTTP, you can modify your start page, automatic opening, and so on. In the FTP, you can modify the open option, the home root directory, and so on.

■ Securing your server

You can restrict access to your site in FrontPage Explorer.

Access authorisation procedures are as follows:

12: Publishing and security

- **Create, administer and explore**. This authorisation allows users to modify, add or delete Web site pages. They can also extend access to others users.
- **Create and explore**. This authorisation allows users to modify, add or delete Web site pages.
- **Explore**. This authorisation only allows users to explore the site pages.

Let us recall now the traditional relations. A Web server contains several sites which are hierarchically structured. There is the Web site root, which is the father, created as the default. The parent site, or root, is the equivalent of the root reader in Windows Explorer. Then, there are the children, or subsites. These are the sites you create in FrontPage. For example, the Impressionists site is a child site of the Web site root of your server.

Access authorisations are also hierarchically structured, meaning that the authorisation granted to the Web site root apply to all the child sites.

■ Testing the Web server

You must test the server, because this is the most practical way of discovering errors or modifications that need implementing.

To test your server in Intranet:

1. Install it on a colleague's computer. Open the browser.
2. Enter your site's address.

    You can view your site on your colleague's computer.

    Make sure that you check all the links, as well as the coherence of your pages.

If you do not know the name of the Web server computer:

FrontPage 2000

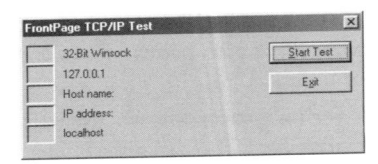

Figure 12.9 The test displays the 'coordinates' of the Web server computer.

1. On the server computer, launch FrontPage. Click on the **question mark** (Help), then on **About FrontPage**.
2. Click on **Network Test**, then on **Start Test** (see Figure 12.9).

The name of your server computer is displayed.

■ Visiting your site

Now that you have created and published your site on your IP server, treat yourself: go and view it on the Web.

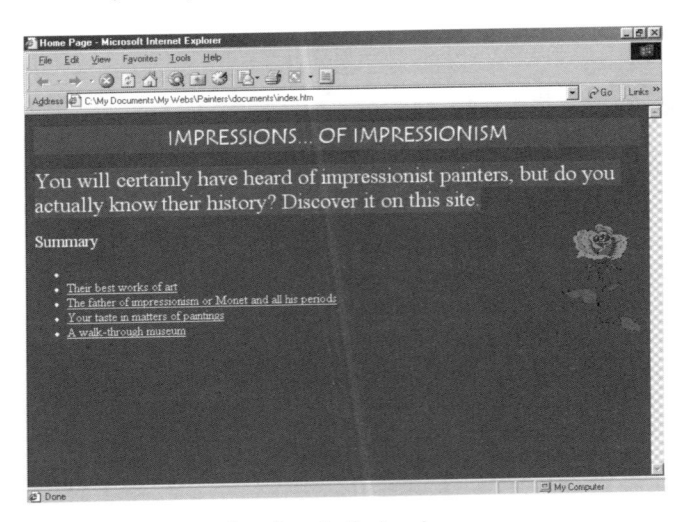

Figure 12.10 Your site Start Page is displayed.

12: Publishing and security

To view your site:

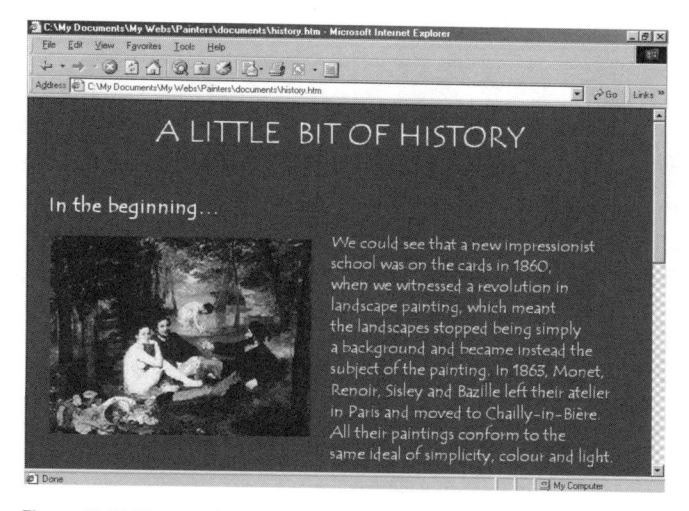

Figure 12.11 History of the impressionists.

1. Launch your browser, then the Internet connection. In the Address box, type your site URL of (see Figure 12.10).
2. Click on **History** to display the page (see Figure 12.11).
3. Click on the rose, then on **Their best works of art** (see Figure 12.12).
4. Click on the rose, then on **The father of impressionism...** (see Figure 12.13).
5. Click on the rose, then on **Your preferences...** (see Figure 12.14).
6. Click on the rose, then on **A walk through the museums** (see Figure 12.15).
7. Close the browser and the connection.

Enjoy surfing the Web and be as creative as you dare!

FrontPage 2000

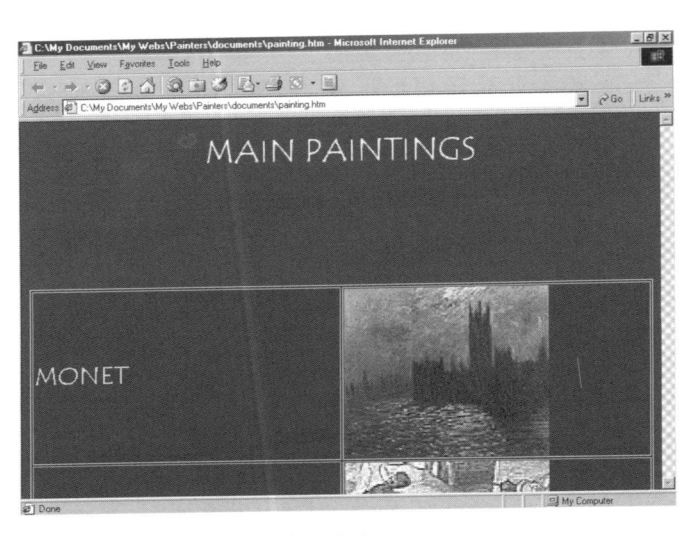

Figure 12.12 Some impressionist paintings.

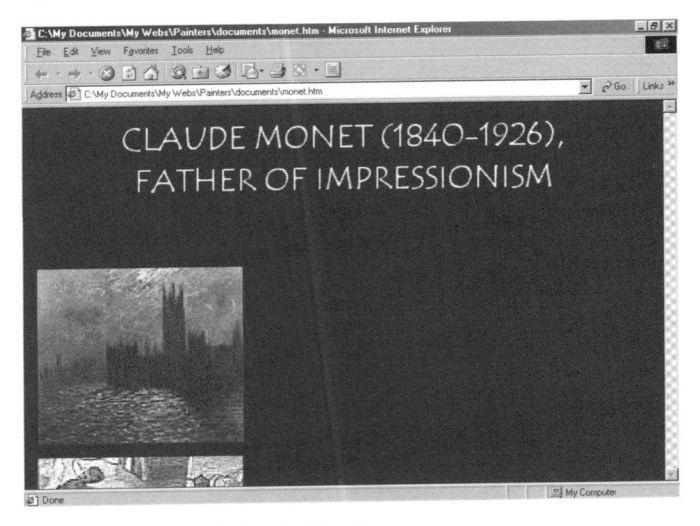

Figure 12.13 Some paintings by Monet.

12: Publishing and security

Figure 12.14 Site questionnaire (form).

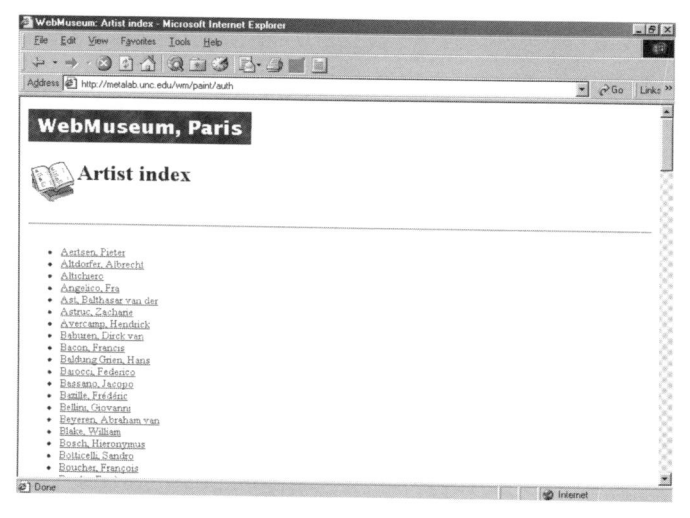

Figure 12.15 Grand Masters Site directory.

Index

A

Accented uppercase, inserting 72
Activating ScreenTips 9
Administrator, configuring 196
Amending text 80
Animated pictures
　inserting 152
　modifying 152
Applying a style sheet 66
Applying borders
　paragraph 98

B

Background
　colour 123
Background
　deleting 125
　other page 125
　picture 126
Blank line, inserting 74
Bookmark
　creating 166
　definition 166
Browser 23
　definition 23
　targeting 64

Bulleted lists
　creating 96
　modifying bullets 97
Bullets, modifying 97

C

Checking, hyperlinks 171
Choosing a subject for the site 36
Clearing
　selection 80
Clearing text 81
Clip Art
　establishing a picture library 107
　finding a picture 106
　inserting a picture 104
　opening 104
Closing
　page 58, 70
　site 44
Colour
　applying to text 90
　create 91
Colouring
　HTML code 29
　hyperlinks 170

FrontPage 2000

Configuring the Administrator 196
Connections
  creating the IP connection 189
  definition 187
  installing
    dial-up networking 189
    TCP/IP protocol 188
Corporate presence wizard 39
Correcting spelling errors 132
Create
  custom colour 91
  new folder 50
Creating
  bookmark 166
  formatting with style sheets 66
  forms 155
  frame 139
  frames pages 137
  hyperlink
    to another page 165
  hyperlinks
    to another site 167
  interactive pictures to another page 166
  IP connection 189
  page 55
    with a template 65
  site
    blank 39
    customer support 40
    from a folder 41
    with a template 39
    with a wizard 39
    with one page 38
  tables 144
  task 182
Customising the tool bar 14

D

Data processing 164
Defining
  frames pages 142
  properties
    frames 141
    pages 140
Delete
  formatting 93
  picture 110
Deleting
  folder 50
  hyperlinks 167
  page 58
  paragraph border 99
  site 45
  task 183
  text 81
Dialog boxes 12
Display
  views bar 18
Displaying
  folder list 54
  Office manager 6
  status bar 16
  tool bar 14
Displaying, HTML mode 24

Index

Downloading the file transfer software 191
Duplicating a line 128

E

Editing text 81
Entering text
  how to 71
  in a page 70
  in a table 146
  inserting accented uppercase 72

F

Field data type 159
Fields 155
Files, list 178
  modified 178
  old 178
  unlinked 178
Finding pictures in Clip Art 106
Folder list
  definition 54
  display 54
Folders
  closing 53
  creating a new 50
  deleting 50
  opening 53
  organising pages 62
  Private 50
  renaming 50
  sorting files 178
    modified 178
    old 178
    recent 178
    unlinked 178
  view site folders 49
Folders, list
  recent 178
Folders module
  closing a folder 53
  definition 18
  display 49
  opening 53
  opening a folder 53
  Private folder 50
Formatting
  applying a border
    paragraph 98
  background
    in colour 123
  background
    picture 126
  bulleted lists 96
  case 89
  custom colour 91
  deleting 93
    background colour 125
    border 99
    text animation 130
  dialog boxes
    Font 92
    Paragraph 95
  font 87
    default 86
  font size 88
  framing
    page 121
  HTML code 28

modifying bullets 97
paragraph alignment 94
paragraph indent 94
procedure 86
reproducing 101
shading
  all paragraphs 122
  paragraph 100
splitting a paragraph 127
table 149
text animation 129
text colour 90
themes 120
using, background from another page 125
Formatting, before printing 59
Forms
  creating 155
  data processing 164
  definition 154
  field 155
  field data type 159
  inserting
    a drop-down menu 161
    command button 163
    fields 156
    multiple-choice options check box 161
    options check box 159
  specifying properties
    of an options check box 160
    of a text box 157
  specifying the properties
    of a command button 163
    of a drop-down menu 161
  text box 157
    scrolling 159
Frames 136
  creating a frame 139
  defining page properties 140
  defining properties 141
  frames pages 137
    defining 142
    saving 143
    testing 144
Frames pages 137
  creating 137
Framing
  page 121

H

Help
  asking a question 31
  contents 29
  index 32
  visiting the Microsoft site 29
  what's this? 33
Help contents
  how to use 30
  opening 29
Help index
  how to use 32
  opening 32
Hiding
  spelling errors 63

Index

tool bar 13
views bar 18
HTML 21
  code formatting 28
  colouring the code 29
  display
    how to 24
    in Normal mode 25
  examples of tags 22
  source code protection 27
  viewing 24
HTML tags 22
Hyperinks
  to another site 167
Hyperlinks
  bookmark 166
  checking 171
  colour 170
  definition 18
  deleting 167
  repairing 173
  specifying 164
  testing 174
  to another page 165
  viewing 174
Hypertext 20
  definition 20

I

Images
  placing 112
  resizing 111
Importing
  pages 175
  site 43
Insert
  interactive picture area 117
Inserting
  accented uppercase 72
  command button 163
  drop-down menu 161
  fields in a form 156
  files 76
  lines 127
    blank 74
  multiple-choice check box 161
  options check box 159
  picture file 108
  pictures 104, 117
    animated 152
    Clip Art 104
  scrolling text box 159
  sound 149
  text 80
  text box 157
Installing
  server 193
  TCP/IP protocol 188
  Windows 98 dial-up networking 189
Interactive pictures, to another page 166
Interactivity with forms 154
IP
  connections 187
  definition 186

L

Language 47

Launching FrontPage
- short-cut icon 6
- using the Programs menu 6
- with Office manager 6

M

Menu bar
- new functions 11
- options 12

Modify
- case 89
- text colour 90

Modifying
- animated pictures 152
- font 87
  - default 87
- font size 88
- site 181
- table 149
- task 183

Mouse, using 9

Moving within text 74

N

Navigation
- between pages 70
- managing pages 180
- organising site structure 179

Navigation bar, specifying names 48

Navigation view
- definition 18

- managing pages 180
- organising the site 179

New
- features
  - of the tool bar 14
- functions
  - of the menu bar 11

New features
- additional tool bars 15
- animating text 129, 130
- answers wizard 31
- automatic spell checking 131
- choosing a language 47
- creating a site from a folder 41
- HTML code protection 27
- Reproducing format 101
- side bar 12
- targeting the browser 64
- views bar 17

O

Office manager, displaying 6

Open
- site 45

Opening
- last web automatically 44
- page 56, 70

Options, menu bar 12

Organising, pages 62, 176

P

Page module 70
  closing a page 70
  definition 17
  navigating between pages 70
  opening a page 70

Pages
  background
    picture 126
  background
    in colour 123
    of an other page 125
  closing 58, 70
  creating
    new 55
    with a template 65
  defining
    properties 140
  deleting 58
    background colour 125
  formatting 59
  formatting with a style sheet 66
  frames 136
  framing 121
  how to enter 71
  importing 175
  inserting
    animated pictures 152
    blank line 74
    Clip Art pictures 104
    files 76
    lines 127
    paragraph 71
    pictures 104
    sound 149
    text 70
  list 178
    modified pages 178
    old pages 178
    pages slow in downloading 178
    recent pages 178
    unlinked pages 178
  managing in the Navigation view 180
  moving within text 74
  navigating between many 70
  opening 56, 70
  organising 176
  placing in a folder 62
  printing 60
  renaming 57
  saving 58
  specifying
    home page 52
  splitting of a paragraph 127
  tables 144
  text background 122
  view before printing 59
  viewing in the browser 61

Paragraph
  aligning 94
  border 98
  bulleted lists 96

deleting a border 99
dialog box 95
indent 94
inserting 71
modifying bullets 97
shading 100
splitting 127
Paragraph alignment 94
Paragraph indent 94
Paragraph shading 100
Personal Web server
Microsoft 193
Personal web server
FrontPage 193
Picture brightness
increase 117
reducing 117
Picture contrast
increase 117
reduce 117
Picture library, establishing 107
Pictures
deleting 110
from file 108
increase
brightness 117
contrast 117
inserting 104, 117
interactive area 117
text 116
moving position a stack 117
placing 117
reduce
contrast 117
reducing
brightness 117
restore 117
retrieving pictures on the Web 111
saving 109
toolbar 116
Placing a picture 117
Placing an image 112
Printing
formatting 59
page 60
print preview 59
site structure 181
Programs menu, launching FrontPage 6
Publishing
downloading the file transfer software 191
view the site 202
with FrontPage extensions 190
without FrontPage extensions 191

Q

Quitting
FrontPage 7

R

Redo an action 81
Removing
buttons from the tool bar 14
Renaming

Index

folder 50
page 57
Repairing hyperlinks 173
Reporting module, definition 18
Reports
  checking hyperlinks 171
  pages slow in downloading 178
  repairing hyperlinks 173
  site summary 177
Reproducing format 101
Resizing an image 111
Restore original picture 117
Retrieving pictures on the Web 111

S

Saving
  frames pages 143
  pictures 109
Saving a page 58
Screen 7
Script, choosing the type 48
Searching and replacing text 130
Securing the server 200
Selecting
  clearing 80
  text 80
Selection
  quick 80
Server properties 197
Servers
  definition 192
  different types 192
  installing 193
  IP 186
  Microsoft personal Web server 193
  properties 197
  securing 200
  testing 201
  uninstalling 193
Short-cut icon, creating 6
Side bar, uses 12
Site 36
  adding a folder 50
  closing 44
  contents of private folder 49
  creating
    customer support 40
    with a template 39
    with a wizard 39
    with one home page 38
  creating from a folder 41
  definition 36
  deleting 45
  a folder 50
  importing 43
  list pages slow in downloading 178
  modifying 181
  open
    quickly 45
  opening 45
    last web automatically 44
  organising pages 176

organising structure 179
printing the structure 181
renaming a folder 50
sorting files 178
  modified 178
  old 178
  recent 178
  unlinked 178
specify
  script type 48
  server language 47
summary 177
targeting the browser 64
viewing the folders 49
Site summary 177, 178
Sound, inserting 149
Specifying
  navigation bar names 48
  properties
    command button 163
    drop-down menu 161
    options check box 160
    text box 157
  script type 48
  site language 47
Spell checking 131
  disabling 63
Spelling 131
  automatic checking 131
  correcting 132
Status bar 16
Style sheets 66
System buttons 8

T

Table borders 147
Tables
  borders 147
  creating 144
  entering text 146
  formatting 149
  modifying 149
Tasks
  creating 182
  deleting 183
  modifying 183
Tasks module
  creating a task 182
  definition 18
  deleting a task 183
  modifying a task 183
Templates
  customer support 40
Templates
  using for a page 65
Testing
  frames pages 144
  hyperlinks 174
  Web server 201
Text
  amending 81
  animating 129
  case 89
  clearing 81
  colour 90
  custom colour 91
  deleting 81
    animation 130

Index

    editing 81
    formatting 93
  font 87
    default 87
  Font dialog box 92
  font size 88
  in pictures 116
  inserting 80
    in a document 70
  moving within 74
  quick selection 80
  searching and replacing 130
  selecting 80
Themes, applying 120
Thumbnail, defining settings 115
Title bar, uses 8
Tool bar
  additional 15
  customising 14
  default 13
  hiding 13
  Removing a button 14
  uses 14

U

Undo
  action 81
Uninstalling a server 193

V

Viewing
  HTML code 24
  hyperlinks 174
  Microsoft site 29
  site folders 49
Views bar
  displaying 18
  hiding 18
  hyperlinks 18
  module
    Folders 18
    Navigation 18
    Page 17
    Reporting 18
    Tasks 18
  uses 17

W

Web 20
  retrieving pictures 111
WYSIWYG 26